CAREER PLANNING
A Developmental Approach

JOHN BARKER
The University of Alabama

JIM KELLEN
The University of Alabama

Merrill,
an imprint of Prentice Hall
Upper Saddle River, New Jersey   *Columbus, Ohio*

Library of Congress Cataloging-in-Publication Data

Barker, John
    Career planning : a developmental approach / John Barker, Jim
Kellen.
       p.   cm.
   ISBN 0-02-305884-6
    1. Vocational guidance—United States. 2. College students-
-Employment—United States.   I. Kellen, Jim. II. Title.
HF5381.B29 1998
650.1—dc21   97–25590
                                                 CIP

Cover art: Diana Ong/SuperStock
Editor: Kevin M. Davis
Production Editor: Sheryl Glicker Langner
Design Coordinator: Julia Zonneveld Van Hook
Production Coordination: Custom Editorial Productions, Inc.
Cover Designer: Susan Unger
Production Manager: Patricia A. Tonneman
Director of Marketing: Kevin Flanagan
Marketing Manager: Suzanne Stanton
Advertising/Marketing Coordinator: Julie Shough

This book was set in Classical Garamond by Custom Editorial Productions, Inc., and was printed
and bound by Courier Kendallville, Inc. The cover was printed by Phoenix Color Corp.

 © 1998 by Prentice-Hall, Inc.
Simon & Schuster/A Viacom Company
Upper Saddle River, New Jersey 07458

Printed in the United States of America

10 9 8 7 6 5 4 3 2 1

ISBN: 0-02-305884-6

Prentice-Hall International (UK) Limited, *London*
Prentice-Hall of Australia Pty. Limited, *Sydney*
Prentice-Hall of Canada, Inc., *Toronto*
Prentice-Hall Hispanoamericana, S. A., *Mexico*
Prentice-Hall of India Private Limited, *New Delhi*
Prentice-Hall of Japan, Inc., *Tokyo*
Simon & Schuster Asia Pte. Ltd., *Singapore*
Editora Prentice-Hall do Brasil, Ltda., *Rio de Janeiro*

Preface

The process of career choice and planning represents one of the most important activities in which you will ever engage. The decisions you make, the goals you set, and the plans you implement during this process will not only determine your degree of career success, but also play a major role in your level of personal happiness. Work is such an integral part of your overall life experience that you cannot effectively separate one from the other. Thus, to plan for a high degree of satisfaction in your personal life, you must work to ensure the same in your professional life.

The unfortunate reality is that too many people give only cursory attention to planning their careers. It is common for many to accept whatever comes their way. This "whatever happens, happens" mentality far too often results in career and personal unhappiness.

This textbook was written to serve as a resource for both traditional and nontraditional college students to guide them, step-by-step, through the appropriate stages of career planning. The text utilizes a three-stage model of career development that assists students in acquiring pertinent information as they progress through their own program of career planning. Herein lies the utility of this text: every participant will undergo an individualized program of career development tailored to his or her particular needs.

The career development model incorporated into this text facilitates progress through these stages:

- Career Guidance and Decision Making
- Developing Employability and Job Readiness
- Job Search

The goal of the career development process for each participant is *successful employment*. This is a powerful concept that implies that a career is something more than just a nine-to-five activity. It means that your work is something you find interesting, enjoyable, rewarding, and consistent with your personal goals. These are the things for which each of us should strive in our careers.

A fundamental concept built into the career development model is the notion that career planning is a dynamic, ongoing process. It is a journey rather than an event. The term *career navigation* is discussed in chapter 5, and it emphasizes this changeable nature of careers. Your ability to navigate through the changes and impediments you will face in your career journey is the key to achieving successful employment.

The text uses a series of outcome questions, designated with the icon, throughout each chapter. These questions are designed to help the reader better understand what information should be acquired in that section. In addition, exercises and discussion questions are offered at the end of each chapter to stimulate thought and conversation. Also, several chapters contain additional individual exercises that help participants work through the various stages by acquiring, organizing, and utilizing information pertinent to that stage.

I would like to express my appreciation to those who assisted in the development of this text. My heartfelt thanks to Linda Sullivan, who invited and encouraged me to begin this project; Kevin Davis, Senior Editor, whose insight proved invaluable in polishing the final product; Lynn Metzger, Editorial Assistant, who was always there to answer my questions and provide helpful information; and Kie Harrison, who provided the illustrations for the book.

I would also like to thank the reviewers of this text who provided valuable suggestions and comments: Therese Marie Crary, Ball State University; Dan Galloway, University of Central Florida; Dale F. Grant, Georgia Southern University; Beatrice Iceman, Kutztown University of Pennsylvania; Ned A. Katterheinrich, Columbus State Community College; Rod J. Merta, New Mexico State University; Aneneosa Okacha, University of Wisconsin, Whitewater; Pamela Park-Curry, The Ohio State University; Mary Lockey Smith, Guilfad Technical Community College; Aaron B. Stills, Howard University; and Patricia L. Wolleat, University of Wisconsin, Madison.

Finally, I want to thank my wife Margaret, for without her this book would never have become a reality. I am forever grateful for her unfailing support, encouragement, and understanding throughout the writing of this manuscript. I owe you much.

                                                                                          John Barker

No career exists separate from a community. We each may work as part of many communities throughout our lives. Exploring and discovering our capabilities and developing and applying ourselves to productive work is a path filled with both joys and frustrations. Our search to find and develop the treasure of our gifts and to cope with our limited capacities is characteristic of peoples' lives in communities all over the planet.

This book is for career seekers. It presents career seekers with methods for gathering and organizing information into a process for increasing insight and effective decision making throughout our work lives. There are many practical elements and exercises to guide the career seeker in preparations essential to successful employment.

Our insights and understanding, both of ourselves and the communities in which we work, will change as time unfolds new realities and the forces of nature drive us to age. Developing our capacities to adjust to and balance these forces, and to cope with circumstances beyond our control, challenges us to remember that the career development process is an ongoing, lifelong process, not a static one-time event.

This book is a collaboration that is the result of a great deal of hard work by my colleague John Barker. John is gifted with pragmatism and seeks focus and clarity in his work and life. He has my respect and admiration for the tremendous effort he put into this writing and for his insistence that I clarify, in practical terms, any ideas I may have contributed to the book.

John and I are focused and passionate about our work. We feel fortunate to have discovered our mutual interest and thankful to be working in a community that enables us to strive to apply and develop our differing gifts to productively helping others in their career pursuits.

We welcome your input to this book. We will be preparing future editions and want to hear from the career seekers utilizing this text. You may reach us at Career Center, University of Alabama, Box 870293, Tuscaloosa, Alabama 35487-0293, e-mail: jbarker@sa.ua.edu or jkellen@sa.ua.edu.

                                                                                          Jim Kellen

Contents

3   SELF-ASSESSMENT   23

4   CAREER INFORMATION   41

5   CAREER DECISION MAKING AND GOAL SETTING   49

Introduction to Career Planning

After completing this chapter you should understand

- *What career planning involves*
- *Why career planning is important*
- *The required outcomes of each stage of the career planning process*
- *What is meant by "successful employment"*

INTRODUCTION

The process of choosing and planning a career ranks as one of the most important events in a person's life. Consequently it is the cause of much worry and stress for many people. An individual going through this process is faced with questions such as, "What kind of work do I want to do?" "Will I be able to find employment if I choose this particular career?" "How do I know I am making the right choice?" The burden of trying to answer these questions can be overwhelming.

Information Gathering Process

Benjamin Disraeli, the former prime minister of Great Britain, once said, "As a general rule, the most successful people in life are those who have the best information." This statement is especially appropriate for you as you go through your career planning process. Acquiring information about yourself, career opportunities, and the relationship between the two will appropriately prepare you to make a good, well-informed career choice. It is accurate, unbiased information that holds the key to your successful career planning program. This text is designed to increase your knowledge of those factors that will affect your career development and help you find answers to the perplexing questions you will face during this process.

Definition of and Need for Career Planning

The term "career planning" can be defined as acquiring and using information about yourself and the world of work to make occupational choices and formulate plans to achieve career goals. Implicit in the idea of career planning is that it is an ongoing process. It is not a once-in-a-lifetime event that one completes never to think of it again. As people mature, their interests, skills, and preferences change. As a result of these changes within the individual, the job that a worker at one time had enjoyed may no longer be satisfying. The characteristics and duties of the job may also change with time, resulting in a less than satisfying work situation. Either of these events can restart the career exploration process (Isaacson & Brown, 1993). For example, a woman may choose to become an accountant and spend several years in that profession. Somewhere along the way she may become dissatisfied because of changes within herself, or changes in the job, or both, and will look to correct the situation by switching careers. This desire for change is very common and happens to most people at some point in their working years. Even those who are satisfied with their job and want to remain are engaging in career planning. Just by knowing that they are happy, they have obviously evaluated their situation and "made plans" to stay put. Consciously or otherwise, they are engaging in career planning.

 Why is it important for college students to spend time in a career planning program?

There is ample evidence showing the need for pursuing career guidance activities at the college level. Many students begin their college years with little information on the broad range of career opportunities that are available and lack the self-knowledge to be able to match their interests and abilities to specific occupations. Statistics show that only about half of all students who enter a college or university graduate from that institution within four years. The other half either drop out entirely or spend part of their college years jumping from major to major, thereby adding additional course work and time to their college years. The cost, both economically and in time spent, can be considerable, and regardless of financial conditions, the time factor has no substitute. The difficulty that many students face in trying to select a major, and the fact that so many drop out entirely, is due in large part to a lack of career direction. These people have information deficits that could be reduced with adequate career guidance (Herr & Cramer, 1991). Not only can this guidance result in a better picture of their career goals, but this sharper focus can provide increased motivation that will help to promote success while in college.

Some may argue that not all college students need career guidance because they made their career choice prior to beginning college and will not benefit from such a program. Although this may sometimes be a valid argument, those who choose not to participate in a career exploration program run the risk of "identity foreclosure" (as cited in Gordon, 1981). This occurs when someone makes a decision before fully exploring his personal values, needs, options, and other factors that will impact his ultimate career success. This type of decision making can have disastrous consequences and can result in a poor career choice. The time spent in a career planning program is cheap insurance compared to the consequences of finding oneself in an unrewarding career.

Spending time engaging in career planning is important for another reason. Your job and your personal life do not exist independently of each other. Your level of happiness in your work will impact your degree of happiness in your personal life. It is difficult, if not impossible, to completely separate your work and your personal life. If you spend eight hours at work each day feeling miserable because you hate your job, that miserable feeling does not just end when you leave work at five o'clock, it carries over into your home life. Conversely, if you are interested and enthused about your work, that positive feeling you have from doing something you love can have a very positive effect on the time you spend away from work. Since your job has this type of impact on your personal life, the importance of making a good choice cannot be overstated. Proper guidance in your career decision making can significantly improve your ability to choose a career that will help you achieve not only your career goals, but your personal goals as well.

Generally speaking, the most valuable dimension to career planning is the development of a realistic understanding of your values and potentials and their relationship to career opportunities. This knowledge of "how to" can be utilized throughout your life to maintain employability and a successful career path.

MODEL OF CAREER DEVELOPMENT

 What steps should be taken in the career planning process?

A major aim of this book is to offer a model of career development whereby you have a step-by-step guide for personal career planning. The model follows a three-stage process of (1) career guidance and decision making, (2) developing employability and job readiness, and (3) the job search process. The outcome of the model is *successful employment*, a concept we will discuss later. Figure 1.1 graphically represents the three steps in the model.

We will present a brief overview of the model here before exploring each of the stages in detail in chapters 3 through 10.

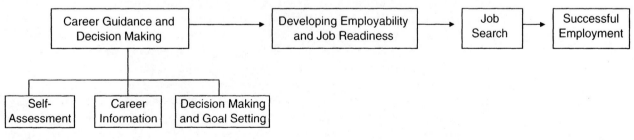

FIGURE 1.1
The Career Development Model

Stage 1: Career Guidance and Decision Making

In the first stage of the model, career guidance and decision making, you will begin to acquire information about yourself and the world of work for the purpose of determining the type of work you want to do. There are three phases in this stage, the first of which is *self-assessment*. The purpose of self-assessment is to allow you to gain insight into the talents, skills, interests, values, and other personal attributes you possess that will be of value in the world of work. This is a critical component of the career development model and is the cornerstone of successful career planning.

Traditionally career guidance counselors focused primarily on providing students with information on different occupations and gave little attention to assessing the internal factors the person would be bringing to the workplace. Most early vocational guidance counselors encouraged students to read about different jobs, and quite often this information was the extent of the counseling process. The belief was that occupational information alone provided sufficient basis for choosing a career (Brown, Brooks, & Associates, 1990). Historically college placement offices existed basically to assist students in finding employment after graduation and placed little importance on the developmental aspects of career planning. Today there is considerable emphasis in the area of career counseling on self-understanding and self-assessment. Most college placement offices have expanded their programs to offer self-assessment and similar developmental programs aimed at those who have not decided on a career (Herr & Cramer, 1991; Tolbert, 1982).

In sum, developing an accurate, objective understanding of the characteristics you possess and the abilities you bring to the workplace is the framework on which to begin formulating your career choice.

The second task in the career guidance and decision making stage is to gather *career information*. The purpose of this phase is to familiarize yourself with the characteristics of particular occupations. In acquiring this information, keep in mind that the more you know about the wide variety of occupational choices available to you, the better prepared you will be when it comes time to make your career choice. Having a broad understanding of occupations in general, as well as a detailed knowledge of specific areas of interest, will place you in an advantageous position for decision making. Many people have stereotypical views and misconceptions about the nature of particular occupations due to a lack of or flawed information. This can have serious consequences if the information is used as the basis for a career choice. It is your responsibility to acquire objective, up-to-date information on potential occupations before you make a career choice.

Occupational information is available from a number of sources, which are discussed in chapter 4. Pertinent information you will need to acquire in this stage for each potential occupation includes (1) the characteristics and working conditions of the occupation, (2) necessary training, degrees, certification, licensure, etc., (3) salary range, and (4) employment outlook.

The third phase of this stage of the model is *decision making and establishing career goals*. This portion of the developmental process represents a turning point in your career planning, because it is here that you actually choose a career and begin to develop tangible goals based on the information you acquired in the first two phases. Many people come to an abrupt halt in their career planning process when faced with the prospect of making this decision. These people postpone their decision because they are afraid of the commitment that goes along with it and they feel uncertain that the choice they make will be the "right" one. This anxiety and indecision can be minimized through a realization that there is no single "right" career for any one person. Everyone possesses a range of transferable skills, giving them the capacity to be successful in many different occupations. Chapter 5 explores the decision-making process as well as the related area of goal setting.

Stage 2: Developing Employability and Job Readiness

The second major stage in the career development process is developing employability and job readiness. To improve your chances of becoming employed in your chosen profession, you will need to acquire the background that employers look for when they hire their personnel. In addition to the proper education, obtaining work experience via volunteering, part-time employment, work-study programs, internships, co-ops, etc., is an excellent way to make yourself more employable. These experiences need not be directly related to a career choice; in fact, these experiences often reveal aspects about your work values, habits, and attitudes which are key to self-discovery. One of the major tasks of this stage is to create a plan to acquire the "employability factors" that will make you more marketable when you begin interviewing for jobs.

Another task to be completed during this stage is learning how to write an effective resume and cover letter. Many times your resume will be the first introduction you will have with a company or organization. While this document alone usually will not secure a job for you, it can definitely remove you from consideration. A poorly written resume with a weak format and/or typographical errors will almost assuredly get you a rejection letter. On the other hand, a good, well-written resume will make a strong first impression and can be your ticket to the job of your dreams. Chapters 6 through 9 address each of the major components of the developing employability and job readiness stage.

Yet another objective of this stage is to prepare yourself for the job search process by sharpening your interviewing skills. Very often an individual will have all of the qualifications for a certain position but will lose out to a less qualified person because of a poor impression during the interview. An effective initial interview is one of the most often cited reasons that companies give for hiring a particular person. During the interview process, your ability (or inability) to adequately convey how you can be of benefit to an employer plays a pivotal role in determining whether or not you will get a job offer. The best education, experience, and skills in the world will not help you if you cannot effectively communicate these to a potential employer during an interview.

Stage 3: Job Search Process

In this final stage of the model, you will be concerned with developing strategies to increase the likelihood of finding a job. You will learn how and where to look for work opportunities that are of interest to you. Knowing which job search strategies are the most effective can take a lot of the frustration out of "beating the bushes."

An effective job search campaign is more than a "hit or miss" proposition where you mail out resumes haphazardly, hoping to receive a positive reply. A good campaign is well-organized, structured, and purposeful. As with any promotional campaign, you will need to locate the target market (desired employers), present them with an appealing product (you), and demonstrate why this product is better than the competition (other applicants). To be successful usually takes more than luck. It takes planning, persistence, and patience, and the results of this preparation will be reflected in the number of job offers you receive. Developing effective job search strategies is discussed in chapter 10.

Developmental Nature of the Model

A key aspect of the model presented in this book is its developmental nature, meaning that the stages should be completed sequentially. In other words, you must complete stage 1, career guidance and decision making, before you can move into stage 2, developing employability and job readiness, since it is obvious that you will need to have made a career choice before you can begin working toward your career goals. Furthermore, both of the first two stages must be completed before you can move into stage 3, implementing a systematic job

FIGURE 1.2
The Cyclical Nature of the
Career Development Model

search, and working toward becoming "successfully employed." Therefore, to ensure preparedness for entrance into each stage you must have adequately addressed all of the components of the previous stage.

Successful Employment

 What is meant by "successful employment?"

The desired outcome of your career development process is *successful employment*. This term implies that you are productively employed in a job that you find especially enjoyable and one that is consistent with your career goals. Compare this with someone who graduates with a civil engineering degree, for example, and unhappily settles for a job unrelated to engineering because she cannot locate anything in her field. This person is *not* successfully employed. The reality is that not everyone becomes successfully employed in their first job, and unfortunately some people never reach this goal. Regardless of the reasons one might find himself unsuccessfully employed, the need for continued career planning and development is ongoing. Inherent in the design of the career development model is that it is cyclical in nature. This means that individuals who are not satisfied with their work situation can return to the appropriate stage and complete the tasks necessary to achieve successful employment (Figure 1.2).

Those who do achieve successful employment have reached the pinnacle of job satisfaction. Successful employment represents a goal that should be pursued with zeal, and you should be satisfied with nothing less. By using the principles and guidelines presented in this text, you will be able to guide yourself through the sometimes difficult, always exciting process of career planning.

EXERCISES AND DISCUSSION QUESTIONS

1. If you had to convince a fellow student that career planning is important for ensuring career success, what would you tell him? Give at least three reasons.
2. Using the career development model as a guide, write a short essay on where you see yourself in the career planning process. What steps, if any, have you already taken in your career development? What do you still have to do?
3. Describe what "successful employment" means to you. How important is it for you to achieve successful employment? What are the consequences of *un*successful employment?
4. Address this question: Do you think most people choose their career through careful, thoughtful planning, or more by chance? Support your position.

Demographics and Workplace Trends: A Legacy of Change

After completing this chapter you should understand

- *How work in America has changed*
- *How the demographics of the workforce have changed*
- *Where we are today as a working society*
- *What the workplace and workforce trends of the future are*
- *What skills will be needed by the worker of tomorrow*
- *How these changes will affect you as a participant in tomorrow's workplace*

INTRODUCTION

As a participant in the workforce of the future it is important for you to gain an understanding of what the workplace is expected to be like. Questions such as, How is the world of work expected to change? and How will these changes affect me? are very relevant for anyone who is in the process of planning their career. To better understand the future of the working world, it is helpful to first look at the workplace of the past. Awareness of past trends and their impact on today's work environment can give you a clearer picture of the future job market and a better understanding of where you see yourself in it. To that end we will offer here a brief history of work in this country before turning our attention to the workplace of the future.

While recognizing the significance that other countries have had on the evolution of work, the information presented in this chapter will focus primarily on the historical development of work in the United States. Attempting to outline the developmental changes in the nature of work for every country is beyond the scope of this text.

CHANGES IN WORK AND WORKERS

The conditions affecting work in America have continually changed since the first immigrants arrived bringing with them their vocational skills and work ethic. The type of work in which Americans have engaged, the workplace, and the makeup of the workforce have evolved and transformed with each passing decade. Likewise, the "typical" American worker has changed significantly from the perspectives of age, gender, culture, education, disabilities, and values (Jamieson & O'Mara, 1991).

 How has work changed throughout the history of America?

Since before America was even recognized as an independent nation and throughout most of the 19th century, most jobs in this country were directly or indirectly related to the growing and distribution of crops and livestock. This agricultural employment base was necessary in order to provide sufficient food for the population. According to U.S. Census Bureau statistics, in 1840 nearly 7 out of 10 workers were employed in farming related jobs (Johnson & Dailey, 1994). As time went by, advances in agricultural technology and increased knowledge of cultivation techniques allowed farmers to produce more food on less land. This profound increase in productivity brought on the beginning of the end of farming as a primary source of employment. By 1900 the percentage of workers in America employed in this area had dropped by nearly half to 37.5% and today only about 2% of the population works in farming related jobs. Figure 2.1 graphically illustrates the decline of farming as a way of life in America over the last century and a half.

With the increasing use of mass production techniques in the second half of the 19th century, the employment base shifted significantly to an industrial workforce which allowed manufacturing firms to begin producing goods in quantities never before thought possible. As the demand for workers shifted to this sector, people began moving away from farms and agriculture-related jobs seeking the "good life" afforded by the wages of the manufacturing industry. This trend continued through the first half of the 20th century and the economy, as a whole, prospered, fortunes were made, and the United States set the standard for manufacturing and industry as it became the richest country in the world.

This industrialized workforce peaked in the middle part of the 20th century as the country and economy continued to evolve. Led by expanding and competing markets, along with increasingly efficient mass production, American companies began to invest more and more money into research and development. This trend led to technological advances, higher levels of worker efficiency and productivity, and ultimately to fewer workers in the manufacturing industries. The second half of the 20th century has come to be known by several names—the space age, the computer age, the information age—all of which reflect the shift in employment to the higher-skill, technology-based world of work

FIGURE 2.1
Percentage of Labor Force
Employed in Farming
Occupations

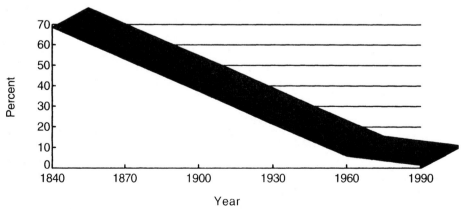

Source: U.S. Census Bureau

in which we live today. A look at the two major employment sectors will help illustrate this shift away from a manufacturing-based workforce to the technological/service-oriented workplace of today.

Changes in Employment by Sector

Most civilian, nonfarm employment in this country is classified into one of two major sectors: *goods-producing* and *service-producing* industries. Goods-producing jobs are those in which the company produces a tangible product. The manufacture of automobiles, appliances, clothing, and consumer products, as well as the construction industry, are examples of this type of employment. Service-producing industries are those which do just that, provide a service. This includes occupational groups such as retailing, financial services, government, and real estate. A study of the relationship between these two employment sectors over the past several decades shows that they are moving in opposite directions.

Goods-Producing Employment.   Goods-producing employment in America increased dramatically as the industrial age began to take off in the 1800s and continued growing through the first half of this century, peaking in the mid-1900s. In 1950, about 40% of all workers in this country were employed in goods-producing jobs (U.S. Department of Labor, November 1993). Since that time the proportion of people who work in this sector has been dropping (see Figure 2.2). Currently only about 20% of the workforce is employed in this sector (U.S. Department of Labor, November 1993).

The last four decades have been lean ones for jobs in the goods-producing sector, and the future looks no more encouraging. Blue-collar positions that previously offered good paying jobs to low-skill, less-educated workers are continuing to be depleted because of the changes in the nature of work (Cetron, 1994). Projections indicate that by the year 2005, the proportion of workers employed in this sector will have dropped to only 17–18% of the labor force (U.S. Department of Labor, November 1993). Some have even predicted that the few remaining unskilled and semiskilled manufacturing jobs will disappear altogether because of new technology in computerized design and manufacturing, robotics, and semiconductors (Cetron, 1994).

Service-Producing Employment.   Jobs in the service-producing sector, on the other hand, have burgeoned since World War II, with the number of workers employed in this

FIGURE 2.2
Percent of (Nonfarm) Workforce
Employed in Goods-Producing
Industries versus Service-Producing
Industries

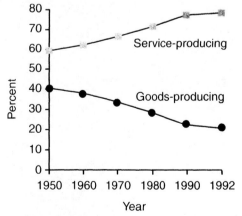

Source: U.S. Department of Labor, *Monthly Labor Review*, November 1993

sector expanding from 22.9 million in 1945 to 85.4 million in 1992 (Johnson & Dailey, 1994)—almost quadrupling in number during this period. As shown in Figure 2.2, service-producing jobs increased, on a percentage basis, from just over half to nearly 80% of the workforce during this time.

The prospects for continued growth in the service-producing sector are equally as impressive, with government forecasters predicting significant increases in both numbers and percent of workforce well into the next decade. Of the projected 25.1 million new (nonfarm) jobs that will be added to the economy between 1992 and 2005, 24 million are expected to be in the service-producing sector (U.S. Department of Labor, November 1993).

These changes can and will have an impact on your career options. As the world of work continues to change, it is important in your career planning to know where you can go to obtain up-to-date information on the projected demand for the specific occupations you may be considering. Reliable sources for this type of information are discussed in chapter 4.

LABOR FORCE GROWTH

 How has the size of the labor force changed and how will these changes impact your career planning?

As the population of the United States continues to grow, the number of people in the workforce in this country also continues to increase (see Figure 2.3). Arguably one of the biggest factors impacting the labor force of today is the "baby boom" generation—those people who were born in America between the years of 1946 and 1964. During this period, 77 million babies were born in the United States—a 50% increase over the previous 18-year period. This population explosion resulted in a flood of people entering the labor force in subsequent years as the baby boomers began to reach working age. During the 30-year period from 1960 to 1990, the United States workforce nearly doubled—an unprecedented period of growth in our nation's history.

The 1970s were an especially expansive period when the number of working people grew by 24 million. This growth spurt was caused not only by the baby boomers who were beginning their careers, but also by women entering the job market in increasing numbers. The old stereotypes that had prevented women from working outside the home began to crumble during this time and women took to the job market as never before. Of the 24 million workers in the 1970s, nearly 14 million, or 58%, were women. Quite a change considering that just a few decades earlier less than 20% of American workers

FIGURE 2.3
The U.S. Labor Force

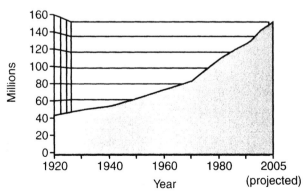

Source: Bureau of Labor Statistics

were female. A more in-depth discussion on the impact of women in the labor force is provided later in this chapter.

SHORTAGE OF WORKERS

The period of labor force growth peaked during the late 1970s and began to decline during the 1980s as the baby boomers grew older and the number of new entrants into the workforce began to decrease. Whereas the labor force grew by 30% during the 1970s, the 1980s saw only a 17% increase—still growing, but not nearly as fast. To further illustrate the slowdown in labor force growth, consider this fact: before the growth rate peaked in the latter part of the 1970s, as many as 3 million new workers per year were streaming into the labor force; by the end of the 1980s, less than 2 million were entering the job market every year. A major contributing factor to the decline in the labor force growth rate has been the decreasing number of young people in this country. The "baby bust" generation—the years after the end of the baby boom when birth rates decreased significantly—has provided fewer entry-level workers in recent years. In fact, in 1990 there were about one-third fewer 18-year-olds in the United States than in 1978. The long-term implications of this trend for employers is clear: a shortage of workers. Fast-food companies, retail operations, and others who normally employ teenage workers have had an increasingly difficult time staffing their operations and have often had to offer incentives in the form of higher wages and more benefits in an effort to entice people to come to work for them.

A book published in the early 1990s entitled *Help Wanted* (Hopkins, Nestleroth, & Bolick, 1991, p. 3) highlighted several examples of how the worker shortage had already begun to impact employers' ability to run their businesses:

- In Hyannis, Massachusetts, owners of a Denny's restaurant had to close up shop at the beginning of the summer beach rush because they could hire only 13 of the 70 employees they needed.
- Disneyland (perhaps the most coveted teenage job site in southern California) was unable to fill 200 of its 2000 jobs.
- At least one state, Connecticut, has been forced to lower the statewide minimum age for most jobs from 16 to 15 in an effort to help businesses hire enough workers.
- A hotel chain had to close two floors of one of its operations because the company could not hire enough housekeepers.

All may not be as bleak as some of these events might indicate. The *Occupational Outlook Quarterly* (U.S. Department of Labor, spring 1992) notes that the number of youths in the labor force will gradually increase after the mid-1990s and by 2005 the number is projected to be 2.8 million more than it was in 1990. This increase in young workers should help alleviate the shortage of entry-level workers that many employers have experienced in recent years.

WORKPLACE SKILLS

Skills Disparity

Another disconcerting workplace trend of recent years is the low skill level of the workforce as a whole. Because of new technologies, the skills needed in the workplace and the context in which they are used are constantly changing (Carnevale, 1991). With the decline of manufacturing and other low-skill jobs, it is no longer realistic for workers with little education or training to expect to find high-paying jobs (U.S. Department of Labor, October 1993). New skills are needed by members of the workforce in order for them to handle the requirements of jobs in today's workplace.

In the mid-1980s, the Department of Labor commissioned a study on the long-term trends in the labor force. The results of the study, known as *Workforce 2000*, projected that a disparity would exist between the skills needed in the workplace of the future and the level of skills that workers would actually possess. This prediction has come true. Employers today not only have difficulty in finding workers, but the workers they do hire oftentimes do not have the skills needed to adequately perform their jobs.

Ironically, even though college degrees are becoming more common, the number of less-educated, lower-skilled people in the workplace is also increasing. The Bureau of Labor Statistics (U.S. Department of Labor, 1994) reports that better than 10% of all workers today do not have even a high school diploma. These high school dropouts, along with the ever-increasing number of immigrants (legal and illegal) who do not possess even elementary math, reading, writing, or verbal skills, add to the pool of low-skill and no-skill workers (Jamieson & O'Mara, 1991). All of this translates into a growing number of workers who do not have the skills needed to compete in today's workplace. Again, from *Help Wanted* (Hopkins et al., 1991, p. 7):

- In recent years, the New York Telephone Company has had to test as many as 60,000 workers just to find 3,000 who were qualified.
- Because of the number of underqualified workers, some fast-food companies have had to "deskill" many of their jobs with measures such as putting pictures of food rather than prices on cash register keys.
- More than one-quarter of the U.S. Army's current recruits are unable to read training manuals written at a seventh-grade reading level.
- Anywhere from 17 million to 27 million American adults are functionally illiterate—meaning they read below an eighth-grade level—accounting for 10–15% of the adult population. To further exacerbate the problem, we are adding 2.5 million functional illiterates to the workforce each year.

Workplace Skills of the Future

Following *Workforce 2000*, the Department of Labor established the Secretary's Commission on Achieving Necessary Skills (SCANS) in the early 1990s. This group was tasked with examining the changing nature of work to determine the type and level of skills needed for employment in the workplace of the future. Not surprisingly, there are major differences between these skills and those that were needed by workers in the past. Figure 2.4 highlights the skills cited by the commission in their report, *Skills and Tasks for Jobs: A SCANS Report for America 2000*, as those necessary for success in the workforce. This information can assist you in your career planning by showing you what will be required, thereby enabling you to develop the skills you will need to compete in the workforce of tomorrow. These workplace skills, and how to acquire them, are discussed in more detail in chapter 6.

The pressing issue for American business is how to deal with the ongoing problem of so many unskilled workers. The solution is to be found, in part, in training. Recent years have seen companies and organizations put more emphasis on employee training programs. Formal company training increased 45% between 1983 and 1991 (Carnevale & Carnevale, 1994), and today companies in America spend about $30 billion per year on training their employees (Reynolds, 1994). This trend is expected to continue, because for many employers these types of programs offer the only means of staffing their organizations with qualified workers.

The following represent those skills that were identified by the Department of Labor as necessary for success in the workplace. The skills are divided into two categories: competencies and foundations. Competencies are the skills necessary for success in the workplace and are organized into five areas. Foundations are skills and qualities that underlie the competencies. These skills and competencies are generic—most of them are required for most jobs. Naturally the degree to which they are needed will vary from job to job.

SCANS Competencies

Competency	How Worker Demonstrates Competency
Resources	Allocates time
	Allocates money
	Allocates material and facility resources
Information	Acquires and evaluates information
	Organizes and maintains information
	Interprets and communicates information
	Uses computers to process information
Interpersonal	Participates as a member of a team
	Teaches others
	Serves clients/customers
	Exercises leadership
	Negotiates to arrive at a decision
	Works with cultural diversity
Systems	Understands systems
	Monitors and corrects performance
	Improves and designs systems
Technology	Selects technology
	Applies technology to task
	Maintains and troubleshoots technology

SCANS Foundations

Foundation	How Worker Demonstrates Skill
Basic skills	Reading
	Writing
	Arithmetic
	Mathematics
	Listening
	Speaking
Thinking skills	Creative thinking
	Decision making
	Problem solving
	Seeing things in the mind's eye
	Knowing how to learn
	Reasoning
Personal qualities	Responsibility
	Self-esteem
	Social
	Self-management
	Integrity/honesty

FIGURE 2.4

Skills Needed for Success in Today's Workplace

Source: *Skills and Tasks for Jobs: A SCANS Report for America 2000,* Secretary's Commission on Achieving Necessary Skills, 1992

EDUCATION AND EMPLOYMENT

 How does educational attainment affect employment?

In addition to on-the-job training, employers are placing more emphasis on formal education. This is especially true of better-paying, professional-level jobs. In the not-too-distant past, it was unusual for someone to continue their education past high school. In 1940 only 5.9% of people age 25 to 29 had graduated from college. At that time it was common to enter the workforce with no college education and still earn a good living. Times have changed. Today about half of all high school graduates attend college, and about one out of four workers obtain at least a bachelor's degree. Let's take a closer look at changes in educational attainment levels of Americans and the impact this is having on the workplace.

Is a College Degree Necessary for Employment in the Future?

As was noted earlier, the number of workers in this country who enter the labor force each year with a college degree has been increasing steadily over the past few decades and this trend is expected to continue for the foreseeable future. At the same time, the Bureau of Labor Statistics projects that the number of new jobs available for people with a college degree is expected to actually *decline* over the next few years. In fact, predictions indicate that in the year 2005, 75–80% of all jobs will not even require a college degree. These circumstances could lead one to question whether or not the time, money, and effort expended in pursuing a college degree is really worth it.

Those who see these figures and conclude that a college degree is not worth the trouble since most jobs will not require one should look beyond these statistics. Further investigation into the differences in employment characteristics between degreed and nondegreed workers demonstrates distinct advantages for the more educated workers. First we will look at income differences.

Degreed Versus Nondegreed Workers. During the period from the late 1970s to the early 1990s, workers who did not graduate from college saw their earnings decrease 30% after adjusting for inflation, while college-degreed workers actually experienced an increase in earning power. Overall, college-educated workers today earn about 60% more than their nondegreed counterparts. Table 2.1 underscores the financial advantage afforded those who finish college over those who do not.

From the perspective of unemployment rates, again, more education offers definite advantages. As shown in Figure 2.5, the worker with no more than a high school degree faces a significantly higher rate of unemployment than his college-degreed counterpart.

TABLE 2.1

Income by Level of Educational Attainment. Median annual earnings of year-round, full-time workers

Educational Level	Earnings
High School	$21,241
Bachelor's Degree	$34,385
Master's Degree	$40,666
Ph.D.	$52,403
Professional	$67,131

Source: Occupational Outlook Quarterly, U.S. Department of Labor, Summer 1994

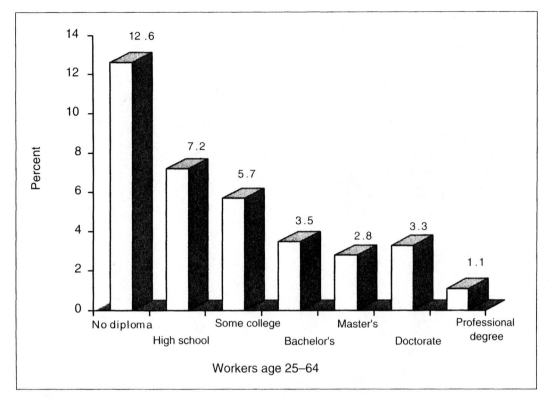

FIGURE 2.5
Unemployment Rates by Educational Attainment
Source: U.S. Department of Labor, 1993

FUTURE OCCUPATIONAL DEMAND

 Which careers are expected to provide the greatest opportunities as we enter the 21st century?

In examining the trends that have shaped the world of work, you should have gained some perspective on where we, as a working society, are today. What then of the future workplace? What will it look like? Specifically, for your career planning, what occupational areas will be in demand? Which ones will experience the most decline? The Department of Labor produces forecasts for the projected increase (or decrease) in demand for workers in many different occupational areas. Table 2.2 illustrates those occupations that are expected to see the greatest numerical growth as we move into the 21st century. Note that of the 30 occupations expected to add the most workers through the year 2005, only 8 will require a 4-year degree. Here again is evidence that the majority of jobs in the workforce of tomorrow will not require a college degree. College graduates need not fret, however; this apparent disparity in the number of jobs that will be available to them is somewhat misleading. The percentage of workers who will have a college degree in 2005 is projected to be only slightly higher than it is today—25%—and the percentage of jobs that will require a college degree is expected to be in the same range.

Table 2.3 focuses specifically on career fields for college graduates. It is apparent that the demand areas for college graduates will be heavily weighted toward the computer science, health care, and teaching professions. This information provides you with a better understanding of the workplace of the future, and knowing the growth trends of possible

TABLE 2.2
Occupations Expected to Add the Most Workers, 1993–2005

	(number in thousands)
Salesperson, retail	786
Registered nurses	765
Cashiers	670
General office clerks	654
Truck drivers	648
Waiters and waitresses	637
Nursing aids, orderlies, and attendants	594
Janitors and cleaners, including maids and housekeeping cleaners	548
Food preparation workers	524
Systems analysts	501
Home health aides	479
Teachers, secondary school	462
Childcare workers	450
Guards	408
Marketing and sales worker supervisors	407
Teacher aides and educational assistants	381
General managers and top executives	380
Gardeners and groundskeepers, except farm	311
Teachers, elementary	311
Food counter, fountain, and related workers	308
Receptionists and information clerks	305
Accountants and auditors	304
Clerical supervisors and managers	301
Cooks, restaurant	276
Teachers, special education	267
Licensed practical nurses	261
Blue-collar worker supervisors	260
Human services workers	256
Computer engineers and scientists	236

Source: *Occupational Outlook Quarterly*, U.S. Department of Labor, Fall 1993

career choices can help you to make a well-informed career choice. Always remember that projections are subject to many variables and change, so it is a good idea to become familiar with how to acquire up-to-date information.

It is apparent that a college degree provides significant advantages to those workers who obtain one over those who do not. Jamieson and O'Mara (1991, p. 24) accurately sum up the differences between the better educated and less educated worker of the future:

> The higher-education end of the spectrum is likely to be a seller's market. The best and brightest are apt to go to organizations designed and operated in ways that are motivating, satisfying, and responsive to this population's needs. The less educated in the work force will struggle to find matches with jobs requiring ever-increasing skill levels, while they compete with an influx of nontraditional workers for the remaining low-skilled, entry-level jobs.

An important point when discussing the relationship between educational attainment, unemployment, and income is that statistics are not absolutes and they can be deceiving. Statistics represent averages and do not take into account individual motivations,

TABLE 2.3
Fastest Growing Occupations Requiring a Bachelor's Degree. Percent employment growth of occupations requiring a college degree, projected 1992–2005

Occupation	Percent Growth
Computer engineers and scientists	112%
Systems analysts	110
Physical therapists	88
Teachers, special education	74
Operations research analysts	61
Occupational therapists	60
Teachers, preschool and kindergarten	54
Speech-language pathologists and audiologists	48
Psychologists	48
Construction managers	47
Management analysts	43
Recreational therapists	40
Social workers	40
Recreation workers	38
Podiatrists	37
Teachers, secondary school	37
Teachers and instructors, vocational education and training	36
Instructors and coaches, sports and physical training	36
Personnel training and labor relations specialists	36
Marketing, advertising, and labor relations managers	36

Source: *Occupational Outlook Quarterly*, U.S. Department of Labor, Fall 1993

interests, hard work, etc. There are many people today with lower levels of education who make more money and are more steadily employed than some with more education. One does not have to obtain a Ph.D. in order to reach the higher income levels and be assured of steady employment. Nonetheless, from a purely statistical perspective, workers with more education are more likely to have higher incomes and lower rates of unemployment than less-educated workers.

WOMEN'S ISSUES

 How has the role of women in the workforce changed?

The Changing Role of Women in the Workplace

Continuing with our discussion of changes in the labor force, we will now turn our attention to one of the most significant changes that has occurred in American labor history: the role of women. At the beginning of the 20th century, less than one out every five women in America worked outside the home and those that did were typically employed in low-paying, nonprofessional jobs (Johnson & Dailey, 1994). This was due in large part to the prevalent societal expectation that a woman's place was in the home acting as wife, mother, and housekeeper.

Dramatic changes have taken place in the role of women in society since that time. As cultural norms and expectations underwent change, women began to seek and acquire jobs outside of the home in ever-increasing numbers. They began to challenge and overcome the stereotypical notions that had prevented them from entering many occupational areas.

During the first half of this century women made only marginal gains in labor force representation. However, beginning in the 1950s women really began to establish themselves in the workplace. In the 30-year period from 1950 to 1980, female representation in the workforce increased from less than 30% to more than 42% (U.S. Department of Labor, November 1993). Even more notable is the fact that over this time the participation rate of women—the percentage of women of working age who hold jobs outside the home—jumped from 33.9% to 51.5%. And as further testimony to the progress women have made in this area, today the figure stands at about 58% (U.S. Department of Labor, July 1994). By comparison, the participation rate of men is about 75%. Bob Snelling, president of one of the largest personnel consulting firms in the country, writes that "The surge of women into the workplace is perhaps the single most outstanding phenomenon of this century" (1987, p. 21).

All of this progress does not mean that women have achieved parity with men in the workplace. On the contrary, women today still make only about 77 cents for every dollar that a man earns (U.S. Department of Labor, 1994b). By some estimations women now represent 43% of all managerial personnel in this country, but still account for only 3% of the top corporate executives (Mahar, 1993).

The reasons for this lag behind men in earnings and status are many. The old, traditional view that women should be the caregivers—supporting wife, mother, homemaker, etc.—while the man "brings home the bacon" has been slow to change. This societal expectation prevented many women from pursuing jobs outside the home.

The lower educational attainment of women, which was the norm until recent years, created a limited number of female applicants for upper-level positions. And not to be overlooked is the fact that women have been the victims of discrimination in the workplace. Many people, even today, hold tight to the "old ways" of doing things. In particular, many older, male workers who have been used to a gender-segregated workplace admit that they are not comfortable with female colleagues (Hopkins et al., 1991). Changing the attitudes of these people about the role of women in the workplace is difficult, if not impossible. As long as there are those in positions of authority who refuse to let go of their antiquated notions and discriminatory practices, there will be limited opportunities for advancement for women. Legislation can serve to help reduce overt acts of discrimination, but until attitudes change, equality for women in the workplace cannot be achieved.

Integrating Traditional Family Roles with Careers

Another work-related issue for women is the subject of child rearing. It is undeniable that women's careers have always been more limited than men's because of the addition of children to a family. For whatever reasons—biological, societal expectations, or others—women have traditionally held the majority of responsibility for looking after their children, especially young children. What impact does this responsibility have on women's work preferences? Apparently a great deal.

About three-quarters of all working women are in their childbearing years. A Gallup poll found that among women with children, half of those polled felt that they could adequately meet their responsibilities to their children if they worked full time, and just 13% wanted to hold full-time jobs with regular hours (Hopkins et al., 1991). These numbers indicate that many women in their childbearing years would prefer options other than the traditional 8-hour-a-day, 5-day-a-week work schedule in order to accommodate both a career and a family life.

Accordingly there is a trend among employers to accommodate working mothers by trying to find solutions to some of the problems they face. Many organizations now offer resources and alternatives to women with children so that they are better able to work. On-the-job day care facilities, work-at-home programs, flextime, and job sharing are all being offered by more and more employers, making it easier for women to work (Cetron, 1994).

As the trend of women entering the workforce continues, more and more women will be faced with issues such as whether or not to postpone having children until later in their careers, or even to forgo having children at all. They will have to address questions such as, Is childcare available? Is it affordable? Would the income from working justify the expense of child care? These are only a few of the issues facing women who choose to work.

Outlook for Women in the Workforce

Looking to the future, women in the workplace should see a continuation of the gains they have made in recent years. The expectation is that by the year 2005, the participation rate of women, that is, the percent of the female population, age 16 and over, in the labor force, will rise to 63% (Cetron, 1994). Furthermore, it is projected that women will comprise almost half of the total workforce by this time; a dramatic increase when compared to the 18.8% figure at the turn of the 20th century.

In addition to the numerical gains, we can expect to see more and more women break through the "glass ceiling" that has historically inhibited their progress up the ladder of corporate America. The lines between "men's work" and "women's work" are rapidly blurring (Hopkins et al., 1991), and as stereotypes continue to disappear, females can expect to become more accepted in the traditionally male-dominated positions. Hopefully with this acceptance the salary disparity that exists between men and women will disappear, and true equity in the workplace can be achieved. Recent trends, as well as earnings projections over the next decade, indicate just that. Between 1983 and 1993 the earnings ratio of women to men increased 10 percentage points, and Marvin Cetron (1994) predicts that by the turn of the century women's salaries will increase to 83% or more of men's salaries. Assuming these trends continue, women's earnings will reach parity with men's in the not too distant future.

MINORITY ISSUES

Individuals from racial minorities face problems and concerns in the workplace similar to those of women. As with women workers, minorities have traditionally been underrepresented in the higher-paying managerial and technical positions. These groups have historically been victims of discriminatory hiring practices, often being denied work just because of their race.

Unemployment and Underrepresentation

The unemployment rate among African Americans, Hispanics, and Native Americans was about twice that of whites when affirmative action and similar equal employment opportunity legislation was introduced in the 1960s. Thirty years later the unemployment rate for these groups is still twice that of whites.

Why does this disparity continue to exist? Farrell Bloch, in his book *Antidiscrimination Law and Minority Employment* (1994), suggests some reasons. First, federal regulations appear to have redistributed minority workers from small and medium companies to larger firms and agencies that are heavily regulated. These organizations recruit and hire minority employees that would otherwise be available to smaller firms, thus their aggregate employment figures are not improved. Second, some employers avoid hiring individuals from groups who are the most likely to file discrimination lawsuits—minorities, women, and older workers. Because statistics show that someone who is currently employed by an organization is significantly more likely to file a discrimination lawsuit than someone who is just an applicant, some employers limit the number of people they hire from these groups. Third, word-of-mouth networking, typically one of the most effective job search methods, can exclude those individuals who have little contact with those who are close to the source. Percentagewise, minorities have low rates of entrepreneurship, hence they are at a disadvantage when it comes to networking and recruiting contacts. For these reasons, and others, affirmative action programs have not had the desired effect of reducing minority unemployment.

Minorities not only face difficulties in getting a job, many find that it is equally, or more difficult, to advance once they become employed. A survey of minority professionals revealed that 40% of African American and Hispanic employees who considered leaving their jobs cited poor career advancement opportunities and a lack of professional development as the major reasons (Martinez, 1995). A common theme among the survey respondents is that minorities don't see other minorities in higher-level positions and therefore believe that their chances for advancement are small.

Anti-Affirmative Action Trends

The mid-1990s saw the beginnings of a shift on the part of the courts, legislative bodies, and in the political arena toward eliminating affirmative action and other racial-preference hiring policies. Amending the Civil Rights Act of 1964 and eliminating the Equal Employment Opportunity Commission are just two of the proposals that have been offered to scale back affirmative action efforts (Wells & Idelson, 1995).

Reverse discrimination lawsuits are challenging employers' affirmative action policies. Whites who feel they are being unfairly treated in the workplace because of affirmative action have been successful in convincing the courts of their right to equal treatment, and winning judgments against their employers. More and more, employers are finding themselves caught in the middle:

> On the one hand, government compliance agents and advocacy groups regularly pressure employers to do more, arguing that their affirmative action efforts are insufficient. On the other hand, groups representing nonminorities often file lawsuits arguing that employers' efforts amount to illegal "preferential treatment" for minorities and/or women (Potter & Youngman, 1995, p. 350).

What effect this trend toward reducing affirmative action regulations will ultimately have on employment opportunities for minorities remains to be seen. Some social scientists believe that equal employment opportunity laws have had little, if any, economic impact on the groups they were intended to help; some have even concluded that they have done more harm than good (Bloch, 1994). Others believe that these programs have been instrumental in helping minorities achieve higher levels of employment. Proponents and opponents will continue to argue the need for affirmative action, and the ultimate fate of these programs remains to be seen.

Areas of Progress

While some of these statistics and trends paint a discouraging picture for traditionally underrepresented populations, there are actually many bright spots in the areas of minority hiring and advancement. Whether as a result of affirmative action/equal employment opportunity policies, changing societal attitudes, or for other reasons, most people believe that discriminatory hiring and advancement practices have decreased since the 1960s when this type of legislation was first enacted (Bloch, 1994; Forrest, 1995). The number and percentage of minorities entering the workforce is growing, and according to the Bureau of Labor Statistics, for the foreseeable future, African Americans, Hispanics, Asians, and Native Americans will all see increases in both their number and percentage of the

TABLE 2.4
Change in Racial Composition of the Labor Force, 1992–2005

	1992	2005	Percent change
White, non-Hispanic	78%	73%	−6.5%
African American	11	12	+9
Hispanic	8	11	+38
Asian and others	3	5	+67

Source: 1994–1995 Occupational Outlook Handbook

total labor force (Table 2.4). Also, statistics indicate that the percentage of management-level positions filled by minorities is increasing, with workers from these populations making significant gains in recent years.

Looking to the future, another reason for optimism among minority workers is the fact that the changing workplace will require employers to hire employees based on their abilities and not their color, gender, or ethnic background. Edward E. Potter and Judith A. Youngman, in their book *Keeping America Competitive: Employment Policy for the Twenty-First Century* (1995, p. 344), note that

> Employers who expect to be competitive cannot afford to restrict their recruitment, hiring, development, and promotions to people from a narrow slice of the qualified labor force. In a nation where the qualified labor pool is broad in terms of race, ethnic background, gender, and in other ways, an employer who is not hiring a diverse work force is very likely not tapping all the sources of talent in that labor pool. . . . This means that while research and debate may continue on the specific value and benefits of work force diversity, the reality is that the workplace is diverse today and that diversity will continue to grow.

With this increasingly diverse workforce will come the challenges of integrating workers from diverse cultural backgrounds, socioeconomic levels, languages, and values. This integration no doubt will be hampered by differing perspectives, communication issues, insensitivity, and ignorance of each others' motivation (Jamieson & O'Mara, 1991). Getting past these obstacles will require the cooperation and understanding of all parties involved, and hopefully a respect and appreciation for other cultures, norms, and lifestyles will come out of this labor force interdependence.

SUMMARY

Work in America is changing at an increasingly faster rate. The agricultural-based economy on which this country was founded gave way to the industrial age, which has since led us to the fast-paced technological age in which we live today. More workplace changes are expected. The method of producing goods and services, the demographic background of the "typical" worker, and the skills needed will continue to evolve. Organizations, as well as individuals, who do not keep up with these trends run the risk of being left behind.

Groups that have been traditionally underrepresented in the workplace have made significant gains in recent years in gaining access to jobs that were previously unattainable. Women and minorities have found that many of the restrictions that prevented them from pursuing employment in certain areas have been eliminated. While there is still much room for improvement, the future looks bright. Projections indicate that both of these groups will see continued gains in workforce representation, as well as access to higher-status, higher-income positions.

EXERCISES AND DISCUSSION QUESTIONS

1. Compare the "typical" American worker of 200 years ago with the "typical" American worker of today. How is he or she different? How is he or she similar? Do these two work for the same reasons?

2. What do you think will be the impact of the increasing number of women and minorities in the labor force? What can management and business leaders do to facilitate the continued progress these groups have made in entering and advancing within their organizations?

3. From the perspectives of income and status in the workplace, women have not yet reached equality with men. To what do you attribute this phenomenon?

4. How will the workforce trends discussed in this chapter—technology, education, gender, and ethnic diversity—affect your career? Will these trends play a role in your career decision-making process? How?

3

Self-Assessment

After completing this chapter you should understand

- *The importance of self-assessment in career planning*
- *More about the characteristics you possess that will influence your career success*
- *How to assess these characteristics and use this information in completing the career guidance and decision-making stage*

INTRODUCTION

Having acquired, in chapter 2, a fundamental understanding of the ever-changing workplace, you are now better prepared to enter your own career exploration and planning program by beginning the first stage of the career development model (see Figure 3.1). The first stage in this model is *career guidance and decision making,* which is actually made up of three phases, or *tasks.* These tasks are:

1. Self-assessment
2. Career information
3. Decision making and goal setting

The purpose of these three tasks is to allow you to acquire information about yourself and the world of work for the purpose of deciding on the type of work you want to do. This chapter focuses on the various components that must be addressed in order to successfully complete task 1, self-assessment. Chapter 4 outlines the steps you should take in completing the career information phase, and chapter 5 focuses on decision making and goal setting.

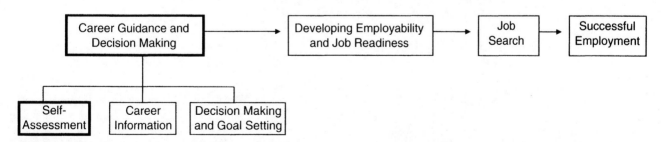

FIGURE 3.1
The First Stage of the Career Development Model—Career Guidance and Decision Making, Self-Assessment Phase

THE NEED FOR SELF-ASSESSMENT IN CAREER PLANNING

 What role does self-assessment play in career planning?

Benjamin Franklin once said, "Three things are very hard—steel, a diamond, and to know one's self." There is a lot of wisdom in these words and quite a bit of relevance to your career planning process. It is not always easy for us to see ourselves objectively. Quite often we see ourselves as we would like to be and not as we really are. But when assessing your personal characteristics for the purpose of career decision making, it is very important that you obtain an accurate, unbiased picture of what you have to offer to prospective employers. Painting an unrealistic picture of yourself can bias the rest of your career planning process. An inaccurate assessment of your skills, for example, can prevent you from seeing how well your true abilities would allow you to perform the job duties in an occupation you are considering. This flawed information can lead to a poor career choice, as well as an unprepared and possibly unsuccessful entrance into the world of work.

It is not uncommon for individuals who are beginning their career development program to neglect the self-assessment phase altogether, focusing their attention on job-related information. The majority of research in this area, however, points to the necessity of building a strong understanding of oneself before making a career choice. Since the early days of vocational counseling the need for self-assessment in career development has been stressed. Frank Parsons, a pioneer in the field of vocational counseling, wrote in 1909 (p. 5) that in wisely choosing a vocation, the first factor to consider is "a clear understanding of yourself, your aptitudes, abilities, interests, ambitions, resources, limitations, and their causes."

More recent research continues to emphasize the importance of self-assessment. In research conducted by the Harvard Business School Club of New York, it was found that there is a high degree of correlation between self-understanding and career satisfaction (Burton & Wedemeyer, 1991). In other words, the people who experience the most fulfillment in their jobs are those who take the time to assess their personal qualities and integrate this knowledge with information on occupational characteristics prior to making a career choice. It is in this self-understanding that the seeds for later career success are sown. Unless you possess an honest and realistic understanding of yourself, the best you can do is to take occupational potshots in the dark and hope you get lucky (Fisher, 1984).

Self-assessment allows you to see where you are now with respect to the skills and background you will need to acquire in order to achieve your career goals. For example, if one of your goals is to become an elected official, and in your self-assessment you determined that your public speaking skills are not up to par for what would be needed in this profession, you can take steps now to become a better speaker. The more effective you are in this area, the greater the likelihood of achieving your goal and being elected to public office. Without a comprehensive program of self-assessment, you may not have become aware of this weakness until it is too late.

 What specific characteristics should you address in the self-assessment phase?

There are several factors that need to be addressed in the self-assessment phase. Some of the most important, and those we will focus on in this chapter, are your *interests* (what you enjoy doing), your *abilities* (what you can do), and your *values* (what is important to you). Another factor that plays an important role in determining how appropriately you are matched with specific careers is your *traits*. Each of these areas are discussed in detail in the following sections.

The desired outcome of this phase is to provide you with an accurate profile of all of the characteristics you possess that will play a role in determining your career satisfaction. You will use this information later, together with occupational information (which is addressed in chapter 4), in order to find a good fit between the two. This idea of *linking*—combining information from the two phases—is a fundamental aspect of successful career decision making. This will allow you to find a strong match between what you have to offer and what a given line of work can offer you in return. A poor match can lead to dissatisfaction and unhappiness, while successful linking can set the stage for a productive, long, and rewarding career.

INTERESTS

The American Heritage Dictionary (1985) defines an interest as "a feeling of curiosity . . . fascination . . . or absorption." There are obvious reasons for assessing your interests in this phase of the career development model. You will want to be sure that the occupation you ultimately choose is something that you find fascinating. You do not want to find yourself in a career that does not appeal to you. By including your interests in the decision-making process, you lessen the likelihood of this happening. Including interest assessment as part of your career exploration begins a pattern that can help to assure career satisfaction. The pattern works something like this:

1. If you choose a job that arouses your curiosity, and you find it fascinating and absorbing, naturally you will be more willing to apply yourself to it.
2. This willingness to dedicate yourself and endeavor to excel will increase the likelihood of your success in that position.
3. The accomplishment, recognition, promotions, money, etc., that you receive as a result of this success can heighten your enjoyment, resulting in an increased level of interest and a desire to succeed which starts the pattern all over again.

This *cycle of success* is the framework for job and career satisfaction and demonstrates the relationship between interest assessment and long-term career success.

A more immediate result of interest assessment is that it can offer initial direction for your career planning. It may be quite easy for you to identify your interests, but it is more difficult to know and understand which occupations will satisfy those interests. For example, if you have an interest in mathematics, you may be unaware that this can lead to satisfying careers in areas as varied as teaching, engineering, research, and accounting. Similarly, a fondness for the outdoors can lead to employment in jobs ranging from forestry to surveying to art, and dozens more. Being able to translate your interests into potential occupations will allow you to begin to narrow your focus of career possibilities.

How to Assess Interests

 How can you assess your interests and begin to tie these interests to career options?

There are a number of methods that can be used to gain a clearer understanding of your interests from an occupational perspective. Some are very simplistic, easy-to-complete approaches that you can do on your own, while others are more detailed, structured methods in which you will need the guidance of a trained professional. Exercise 3.1, Interest Assessment Inventory, is an example of a self-administered assessment instrument that offers a quick and easy way to gain a basic understanding of your interests (see Exercise 3.1 at the end of this chapter). This exercise guides you into the process of "linking," introduced earlier in this chapter, whereby you begin to look for themes or "interest clusters" that will allow you to link your interests to specific occupational areas. Successful completion of this type of exercise can help bring your career choice into sharper focus. The interest assessment inventory, and similar assessments, are basic, nonstandardized instruments. Their strength is in their simplicity of administration and interpretation.

There are also several standardized "tests" that can be used in interest assessment. The term "tests" is used rather loosely because these are not true tests in that you can pass or fail, but are instruments that help you to gain a better understanding of your occupational interests. One of the most popular of this type of assessment tool is the Self-Directed Search published by Psychological Assessment Resources, Inc. This instrument is based on the theory of career development proposed by John Holland, which espouses that individuals, as well as occupations, share characteristics that can be classified into one or more of six different categories. The theory states that the higher the degree of match between the characteristics of the worker and the characteristics of the job, the higher the likelihood of job satisfaction.

The Self-Directed Search is just one of several standardized assessment instruments that are available to help you gain a stronger understanding of the relationship between your interests and the world of work. The professionals in your college or university's career planning and placement office can direct you to those that are available on your campus.

Interest assessment is critically important in career planning, and regardless of whether you choose to use the exercises in this chapter or the standardized inventories, or both, be certain that you allow time in your career planning process to adequately address this aspect of self-assessment.

ABILITIES

An ability is "the quality of being able to do something" (*American Heritage Dictionary*, 1985). From a career planning perspective, your abilities can be divided into two categories: talents and skills. *Talents* emphasize the inborn ability of an individual and are oftentimes associated with areas such as athletics or the arts, but can refer to a variety of different areas. A *skill,* on the other hand, implies something that has been acquired or developed. We usually associate this type of ability with one that has been developed through practice rather than inherited through genetics. While representing different types of capabilities, these terms are, nonetheless, very similar in scope and are key determinants of your career success, and should be evaluated during your self-assessment program.

As with your interests, it is imperative for you to be able to link your abilities with characteristics of different types of work. If you have artistic ability, for example, what jobs are available that will offer you the opportunity to use your talent? Of these, which will offer you the most job satisfaction? Which will offer you the most money? Is it even important for you to be able to use this talent in your career? Questions such as these will enable you to see more clearly what you have to offer the world of work, and equally as important, what it has to offer you.

How to Assess Abilities

 How can you assess your abilities and begin to tie these abilities to your career options?

Your Personal Information Inventory, Exercise 3.2 (at the end of this chapter), is a great place to begin assessing your abilities. By looking at your previous jobs, activities, awards, etc., you can see those areas in which you have a demonstrated proficiency. It may have been that you were in a math honor society, or voted president of the Student Government Association, or you may have won sales awards at a retail store where you worked. Any and all of these accomplishments can offer insights into your abilities and begin to point you toward a potential career choice. Exercise 3.3, Skills Rating Form (at the end of this chapter), offers another method to help you gain a better understanding of your talents and skills. By rating yourself in each of the areas listed, you can get a fairly accurate picture of where your strengths lie. Remember though that this profile is only as good as the information you put into it. Honestly and objectively rating yourself is very important so that you get an accurate appraisal of your abilities. As you work through the interpretation section, hopefully you will begin to see yourself from a new perspective and possibly gain valuable insight into who you are and what you have to offer the world of work.

A secondary outcome of this exercise is that, in addition to your strengths, you may also see your limitations. Be aware that if you do begin to recognize areas of weakness, this does not necessarily mean that jobs which require that particular ability are unattainable for you. Weaknesses can be turned around and used as goals for improvement. By identifying your deficit areas, you can create a plan of action designed to assist you in acquiring those skills that are necessary for success in your chosen profession.

VALUES

Of the many components of self-assessment, probably the most overlooked is the impact of your values on your career choice. Although you may not even be aware of it at the time, your values play a big role in your decision to pursue a specific line of work. By answering the question, "What do I want out of a career?" you can begin to see the role your values play in your career choice because your answers will typically be a function of your value system. For instance, if one of your values is a desire to help others, in all likelihood your career choice will reflect this and you might find yourself in a job such as teaching, medicine, social work, or one of the other helping professions.

It is also important to realize that those jobs that you have already eliminated from your list of potential careers may have been ruled out because of your value system rather than due to a lack of abilities or interest. For example, students who rank financial security as one of their top-most values will, in all likelihood, eliminate certain careers that they perceive "just don't pay enough." These occupations have been rejected because they are not consistent with the student's values. The better you understand your own values, the greater your chances will be of choosing a career that will satisfy those values.

Most people, when deciding on a career, do not consciously think, "Is this occupation consistent with my values?" But when pressed into looking at the underlying reasons for their interest (or lack of interest) in a particular occupation, these individuals will typically reveal one or more of their values. Consider the following exchange between a career counselor and a college student:

Counselor: *"So, what type of work do you think you would be interested in doing?"*

Student: *"I think I would like to go into forestry."*

Counselor: *"What interests you about this line of work?"*

Student: *"I don't know. I've just always thought it would be fun."*

Counselor: *"But, why do you think it would be fun?"*

Student: *"It just seems like an enjoyable job."*

Counselor: *"I'm not letting you off the hook that easily; what aspects of this kind of work seem enjoyable to you?"*

Student: (pause) *"The most appealing thing would be to be able to work outdoors. The beauty of the forest . . . nature . . . animals . . . I can think of no better place to work."*

Obviously, appreciation of the aesthetic beauty of nature is a value to this student. In all likelihood, he has never really thought of his appreciation of the outdoors from the perspective of being one of his values; he just knows that he likes the outdoors.

We are all guided and motivated by our values. Unfortunately we seldom take the time to try and understand how they fit into our careers. Improving your understanding of this important aspect of your personality can help you choose an occupation that is consistent with your values and improve your chances for a fulfilling career.

 How can you acquire a better understanding of the values you possess and gain insight into how they will impact your career choice?

A number of different standardized assessment instruments have been developed that can help you better understand your own values. The Values Scale is one such example. This instrument, and others like it, can be very helpful in assisting you in determining what is important to you, and incorporating this information into your career choice process. Ask at the career planning and placement office on your campus about the availability of this or similar values assessment instruments. However, you do not necessarily have to take a standardized test in order to gain a better understanding of your values. Exercise 3.4, Work Values Assessment (at the end of this chapter), offers you a simple, yet very revealing method of values assessment. In this exercise you will rate different work-related values on their level of importance to you. By doing so, you can develop a better understanding of your own value system, allowing you to see, maybe for the first time, those factors which are important to you in a career.

TRAITS

"She is very outgoing." "He is extremely organized." "She is a hard worker." Statements such as these reveal how other people see you and can give you a glimpse into those characteristics that define the type of person you are. The many aspects of your personality that cause you to act, respond, behave, or just "be" a certain way can be loosely grouped into a classification called *traits*. These are the personal attributes that you possess and which other people use in developing their impression of you.

Your personality traits will play a role in determining how happy and successful you will be in a given job. Ultimately you want to be sure that your career choice is not inconsistent with your personality traits. For example, if you know that you are an extrovert, and interacting with people is something that is important to you and something you will look for in a job, it is unlikely that you would be happy in any job that isolates you from others. Conversely, if independence and working alone are important to you in a job, as it is with many introverts, it is likely you would be uneasy in a job that requires a lot of interaction with others, such as sales or public relations. As another example, if you are a natural leader and enjoy taking charge of situations, it would behoove you to find employment in a job that will allow you to utilize this trait.

In addition to examining your traits to assist in career decision making, it is also invaluable that you identify and demonstrate your marketable traits during a job interview. Oftentimes it is these characteristics that play the biggest part in an employer's hiring decision. For example, a sales manager may hire the person whom he perceives to be the most articulate, believing that this trait is vital for successful sales representatives. Other managers may look for traits such as decisiveness or dependability or even a certain "look." For some employers these characteristics are more important than other, more quantitative factors such as grade point average or the number of years of experience. Some of your traits will be apparent to the interviewer without you having to point them out, such as courtesy, optimism, and enthusiasm. Others may not be so readily apparent, in which case you should be prepared to illustrate your marketable traits by citing examples of how you have demonstrated these characteristics. Consider the following answers from students to a recruiter's question during employment interviews:

> I feel that my leadership ability is demonstrated by the fact that I was elected for two terms as president of one of the largest student organizations on campus.

> My dependability is demonstrated by the fact that I have not missed a single day of work in the past two years.

You can see from these examples that it is more compelling to give specific examples that demonstrate your positive traits than to merely claim that you possess that characteristic. A self-assessment program that includes an evaluation of your traits will help ensure that you can effectively portray desired traits to a potential employer.

How to Assess Your Traits

 How can you gain a better understanding of your traits and how they will impact your career choice?

An easy way to begin to assess your traits is to compile an inventory by listing on a sheet of paper as many words as you can think of that describe you. It is important that you remain as objective as possible, describing how you really see yourself rather than how you would like to be. It may be a good idea to have someone who knows you well look at your list and offer feedback on it. They may be able to provide insight into blind spots of which you are unaware. By putting down on paper these self-descriptive terms, you can begin to form a complete picture of yourself and your traits. This picture can help you to gain a better understanding of the personal characteristics you possess and how they will benefit you in potential careers. Exercise 3.5, Personal Traits Inventory (at the end of this chapter), will lead you through this process.

For a more structured assessment of your traits, you may want to take the Myers-Briggs Type Indicator (MBTI). The MBTI is based on the belief that we can each be classified into 1 of 16 different personality *types*. Each type is determined by one's natural predispositions in four basic areas of human functioning. These areas are (1) how we interact with the world and where we direct our energy; (2) the kind of information we naturally notice and remember; (3) how we make decisions; and (4) whether we prefer to live in a more structured or a more spontaneous way. This assessment tool can provide considerable information on those characteristics that comprise your personality, and can help you to acquire a more solid perspective of yourself for career planning purposes. Taking the MBTI will require the guidance of someone trained in its administration. Check with your college's career planning and placement office or counseling center.

COMPUTERS AS AN ASSESSMENT TOOL

Computerized career guidance systems are available that incorporate self-assessment with occupational information to help individuals through a career decision-making and planning program. Two of the most widely used computer-aided career guidance systems are SIGI Plus (Educational Testing Service) and Discover (American College Testing) (Baier & Strong, 1994). An individual using these programs responds to a series of questions and exercises which the program uses to make recommendations for possible areas of career exploration. Most people find these programs an easy-to-use and enjoyable method of self-assessment and career guidance.

SUMMARY

Having completed this chapter and its exercises, you should now have a clearer picture of yourself and what you have to offer to potential employers. This knowledge will prove very important for two reasons. First, you can now take what you have learned about yourself and combine it with the insight revealed in the next stage—career information—in determining your occupational choice. Second, this self-knowledge will help you to do a better job of selling yourself to potential employers. The more you know about yourself, your abilities, interests, values, and personal traits, the better able you will be to effectively present your strongest attributes during an interview. As you can plainly see, this phase of your career development process can play an integral part in your ultimate career success.

EXERCISES AND DISCUSSION QUESTIONS

1. Suppose you had to give a speech explaining the need for self-assessment in career decision making. What would you say? Give at least three solid reasons why self-assessment is important in career planning.
2. How can the process of exploring one's values lead to a more productive career?
3. From a career planning perspective, what is meant by "linking"? How can it facilitate career success?
4. Which of these two aspects of your personality will play a bigger role in your career choice—your interests or your values? Take a position and defend it.
5. If you were an employer, what general personality characteristics would you look for in hiring your employees? Create a profile of the ideal candidate. How closely does this profile resemble you? Where are you lacking? Can you develop these deficit areas? If so, how? Would you hire yourself?

Exercise 3.1   Interest Assessment Inventory

Identifying those things you enjoy doing can lead you to a discovery of *occupational* interest areas. Using the scale below, rate the degree to which you enjoy, or believe you would enjoy, each of the activities. For those activities that you rate 4 or 5, try to gain an understanding of exactly what it is you like about that activity and, by completing the interpretation, begin to look for possible links to occupational areas.

Interest Level

1	2	3	4	5
Low Interest		Moderate Interest		High Interest

_____ Acting	_____ Chemistry
_____ Creating artwork	_____ Reading technical journals
_____ Writing	_____ Statistical analysis
_____ Designing clothes	_____ Charitable work
_____ Playing music	_____ Psychology
_____ Reading	_____ Working with disabled people
_____ Graphic design	_____ Teaching
_____ Decorating	_____ Politics
_____ Photography	_____ Legal issues
_____ Ballet	_____ Leading a group discussion
_____ Singing	_____ Supervising others
_____ Mechanical repairs	_____ Keeping up with business trends
_____ Working outdoors	_____ Performing record-keeping duties
_____ Operating machinery	_____ Biology
_____ Woodworking	_____ Studying nature
_____ Operating power tools	_____ Selling merchandise
_____ Plumbing repairs	_____ Scientific experimentation
_____ Hunting	_____ Playing team sports
_____ Forestry	_____ Scientific research
_____ Surveying	_____ Public speaking
_____ Geology	_____ Planning events
_____ Meeting people	_____ Visiting new places
_____ Studying languages	_____ Observing human behavior
_____ Studying stocks and investments	_____ Studying religion
_____ Helping others with problems	_____ Learning how things work
_____ Studying artifacts	_____ Caring for sick people
_____ Supervising recreational activities	_____ Doing research

_____ Conservation activities   _____ Doing electrical work

_____ Working with children   _____ Working with the elderly

_____ Studying animals   _____ Botany

_____ Laboratory experiments

_____ Gardening   Other activities:

_____ Aviation/flying   _____ _____

_____ Computers   _____ _____

_____ Mathematics   _____ _____

Interpretation

In reviewing your interest assessment do you see any trends? _____
_____
_____

Do any of the activities listed here stand out as especially strong interest areas? _____
_____
_____

_Does your interest assessment offer any insights about possible careers or point toward
any specific occupational groups you feel you should explore in more detail? If so, list the
occupation(s)_ _____
_____

**_Keep this exercise and use the results in completing Exercise 5.1, Decision-Making Grid,
in chapter 5._**

Exercise 3.2   Personal Information Inventory

This form is used to help organize information on your education, work experience, and other personal information. By compiling this information into a concise format, you may see more clearly where you have focused your energies in the past. These previous patterns of behavior can be used to begin formulating areas of occupational interest. Be as accurate and honest as possible in assessing your likes, dislikes, interests, and abilities.

Name:_____

Education

Name of School	City/State	Years Attended	Degrees Earned
_____	_____	_____	_____
_____	_____	_____	_____
_____	_____	_____	_____

Favorite Courses: _____

_____

_____

Least Favorite Courses:_____

_____

_____

Honors/Accomplishments/Extracurricular Activities:_____

_____

_____

Work Experience

List all of your work experience, paid or volunteer, and rate each on how much you enjoyed that job (most recent experience first).

1. Name of company: _____
   Your title: _____
   Duties:_____

   _____

	1	2	3	4	5
	Disliked		Neutral		Enjoyed

2. Name of company: _____
   Your title: _____
   Duties:_____

   _____

	1	2	3	4	5
	Disliked		Neutral		Enjoyed

3. Name of company: _____
   Your title: _____
   Duties:_____
   _____

	1	2	3	4	5
	Disliked		**Neutral**		**Enjoyed**

Use another page to list additional jobs and use the same rating system.

Abilities and Interests

List any special abilities, interests, hobbies, or talents that you possess (i.e., computers, mechanical aptitude, writing, etc.)

_____

_____

_____

_____

Interpretation

In reviewing your Personal Information Inventory Form, what trends do you see? _____

_____

_____

What areas of your education have been the most interesting? _____

_____

_____

*Which jobs gave you the highest level of satisfaction? Why?*_____

_____

_____

*What kinds of activities just seem to fit you?*_____

_____

Do your background, abilities, interests, etc., offer any insights into possible careers, or point toward any specific occupational groups you feel you should explore in more detail? If so, list the occupation(s). _____

_____

_____

Keep this exercise and use the results in completing Exercise 5.1, Decision-Making Grid, in chapter 5.

Exercise 3.3   Skills Rating Form

This form is designed to assist you in acquiring a better understanding of your skills. By identifying your skill areas, you can begin to link them with potential careers. Using the given scale, rate each of the following skills as you feel they apply to you. For each skill rated 4 or 5, give at least one example of how you have demonstrated your proficiency in that area.

Skill Level

1	2	3	4	5
Low Ability		Moderate Ability		High Ability

Skill	*Rating*	*Example*
Athletics	_____	_____
Analyzing	_____	_____
Writing	_____	_____
Creativity	_____	_____
Management	_____	_____
Communication	_____	_____
Motivating others	_____	_____
Teamwork ability	_____	_____
Persuading	_____	_____
Problem solving	_____	_____
Foreign language	_____	_____
Organization	_____	_____
Instructing	_____	_____
Supervising	_____	_____
Critical thinking	_____	_____
Planning	_____	_____
Research	_____	_____
Interpersonal relations	_____	_____
Time management	_____	_____
Artistic talent	_____	_____
Mathematics	_____	_____

Interpretation

Do you see any trends? _____

Do any skills stand out as particularly strong? _____

In what areas would you like to improve? _____

_____

*Do your skills offer any insights into possible careers or point toward any specific oc-
cupational groups you feel you should explore in more detail? If so, list the occupation(s).*

_____

_____

***Keep this exercise and use the results in completing Exercise 5.1, Decision-Making Grid,
in chapter 5.***

Exercise 3.4   Work Values Assessment

Using the given scale, rate each of the following work values according to the importance you attach to each. Consider how important it is for you to be able to satisfy that particular value through your job.

1	2	3	4	5
Little Importance		Somewhat Important		Very Important

_____ Flexibility   _____ Independence

_____ Location   _____ Stability

_____ Variety   _____ Helping others

_____ Friendship with colleagues   _____ Making decisions

_____ Artistic freedom   _____ Supervision

_____ Low pressure   _____ Responsibility

_____ Power/authority   _____ Teamwork

_____ Security   _____ Public contact

_____ Recognition   _____ Money

_____ Challenging   _____ Mental stimulation

_____ Physically challenging   _____ Competition

_____ Exciting   _____ Prestige

_____ Environmental concerns   _____ Personal growth

Others:

_____ _____   _____ _____

_____ _____   _____ _____

Interpretation

Do any of these values stand out as particularly strong? Which ones? _____

_____

Does this inventory offer any insights as to what you see as important in choosing a career? Elaborate. _____

_____

Keep this exercise and use the results in completing Exercise 5.1, Decision-Making Grid, in chapter 5.

Exercise 3.5   Personal Traits Inventory

Make a list of the traits that describe you (i.e., analytical, people-oriented, aggressive, etc.). Categorize these traits by the degree to which you exhibit the trait using the scale given. For example, if you are extremely *outgoing*, place a 3 by the term to show that you exhibit that trait to a high degree. If *mathematics ability* describes you enough so that you feel it should be on your list, but does not rank as one of your strongest traits, place a 1 by it. Traits that you feel are not characteristic of you at all should not be listed. Each of the terms you list should be at least somewhat descriptive of you; this ranking offers a picture of the relative degree to which you possess each trait.

If you get stuck, ask yourself questions such as, "As a student I am . . .," "As a worker I am . . .," "As a friend I am . . .," etc. For more insights into your personality traits, have a family member or someone else who knows you well make suggestions for your list. This should help to expand your list of personal traits and also lend a degree of objectivity to the assessment.

	1		2	3	
	Moderately Descriptive			Highly Descriptive	
Trait		*Rating*	*Trait*		*Rating*
_____	_____		_____	_____	
_____	_____		_____	_____	
_____	_____		_____	_____	
_____	_____		_____	_____	
_____	_____		_____	_____	
_____	_____		_____	_____	
_____	_____		_____	_____	
_____	_____		_____	_____	
_____	_____		_____	_____	
_____	_____		_____	_____	
_____	_____		_____	_____	
_____	_____		_____	_____	
_____	_____		_____	_____	

Interpretation

Which traits stand out as particularly strong? _____

_____

Which of these traits do you believe will be an asset in your career? _____

_____

Which of these traits do you believe could be a liability? _____

_____

Does this exercise offer any insights as to potential occupations? _____

_____

Keep this exercise and use the results in completing Exercise 5.1, Decision-Making Grid, in chapter 5.

Career Information

After completing this chapter you should understand

- *What the major sources of occupational information are*
- *How to use people as a resource for occupational information*
- *How occupational information should be used in your career planning*

> *Knowledge is of two kinds. We know a subject ourselves or we know where we can find information upon it.*
>
> –Samuel Johnson (1709–1784)

INTRODUCTION

Samuel Johnson's quote relates quite well to the career information phase (see Figure 4.1) of the career development model. Most people, by the time they reach college age, have acquired information on at least some of the many different occupational areas. Few people, if any, however, are knowledgeable of all occupations. The important thing is to know where to find the information you need to successfully complete this phase.

SOURCES OF CAREER INFORMATION

Think back for a moment to your childhood and your earliest thoughts on what you wanted to be when you grew up. Where did these ideas come from? What were the influences that formed your perceptions of work? Finally, how much impact did these early ideas have on your ultimate career choice?

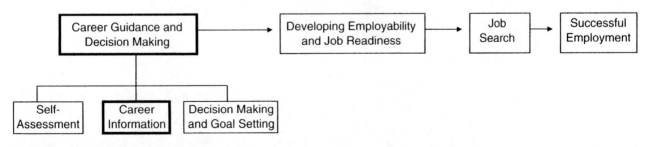

FIGURE 4.1
The Career Information Phase

In the early developmental years, the major influences on children's ideas about work come from their families. Children first begin to acquire information about work, and its role in life, by observing and asking questions about what their parents and other family members do at work. Also, during these formative years, they see and learn about jobs from reading and watching television and films. And while Hollywood may not be the best, most objective, source of career information, it introduces children to characters who are employed in a wide variety of occupations and allows them to learn more about those professions.

As children grow they learn more about different types of jobs and begin to envision themselves in careers that sound interesting and exciting. The occupations that they choose during this time are often glamorous and exciting jobs such as actor/actress, singer, police officer, pilot, etc. Donald Super, one of the foremost authorities in the area of career development, refers to this time in a child's development as the "fantasy" phase (Isaacson & Brown, 1993), where choice of careers is based more on impractical desires rather than on realistic, mature, decision making. Usually these ambitions are transitory and are quite different from the child's ultimate career choice.

As maturing children reach their teenage years, they gather more and more information on occupations from teachers, friends, their parents, and other acquaintances who teach them about work. Reality also begins to take hold during the adolescent years as the maturing child realizes that his early vocational choices may not be feasible. The junior high and high school years can be a very confusing time for students as they seek to answer the question, "What do I want to do with my life?" As they reach college age, students are ultimately faced with the prospect of having to declare their occupational intentions by choosing a major course of study. Many do so without adequate research into the myriad possibilities available to them.

College students who are embarking on a career planning program need to acquire accurate, unbiased information on the characteristics of potential occupations. This information helps the student determine which occupations would be viable career options. Relying on old information sources from their childhood can taint the decision-making process.

Gathering career information in this phase not only increases students' knowledge of possible careers, but also provides the opportunity to see how compatible their values, interests, abilities, and other traits are with these occupations. Generally speaking, the closer your personality characteristics match the characteristics of a certain job, the more likely it is that you will find satisfaction in that job. It should be obvious that obtaining accurate, unbiased information on job characteristics, duties, salaries, etc., in each career field that you are considering is of paramount importance. This type of information is needed for a well-informed career decision.

 How can I learn more about the characteristics of different occupations?

Where should you look for comprehensive, up-to-date information on specific occupations? There are two major sources for this kind of information: people and publications.

People as a Source of Career Information

A wealth of information can be obtained from talking to people who have experience in an occupation that you are interested in exploring. These individuals can give you insight into not only the general duties associated with the job, but also the "behind the scenes" information that may not be common knowledge to people outside of the profession. One of the best ways to tap into this information base is through informational interviewing (Exercise 4.1, at the end of this chapter). In completing this activity, you will obtain the name of someone who is employed in or is knowledgeable of an occupation that is of interest to you, and gather information from him about his job. This offers you a perspective on the occupation from someone who has firsthand experience and can tell you the pluses and minuses of working in that field.

Before you seek out someone for an informational interview it is good to have a fundamental idea of what the job is about. It is recommended that you spend at least a little time in researching the occupation prior to the interview. This preliminary research can help you prepare questions for the interview. Check out some of the occupational information resources listed in the next section to help you with this.

In completing an informational interview you will first contact someone who is currently employed in an occupation that you are interested in learning more about, and either conduct a telephone interview or ask for a face-to-face meeting. When you make contact with this person, be certain to clarify the purpose of your interview, which is to gather information to assist you with your career decision making. Generally people will be flattered that you have chosen to call on them, and their expertise, for assistance. Let them know that you will only need a few minutes; they will be much more likely to help if they know that you are not planning to take up much of their time.

Before you actually begin the interview, be sure to have a list of questions that you want answered concerning the occupation. Use the questions listed in Exercise 4.1 as a starting point, but be sure to include any additional questions that may be of importance to you in making your career choice. Remember that you promised not to take up much of the person's time, so limit your question and answer session to an appropriate length of time. Let the person you are interviewing be the guide; if he is willing to take 30 minutes to an hour with you, gratefully accept his hospitality and use the time wisely. But a good informational interview can take place in as little as 15 minutes, and you can even learn a lot in a 5-minute telephone conversation. Keep in mind that the people whom you interview are doing you a favor, and you need to let them know that you appreciate their time. If appropriate, you may even want to drop them a thank you note in the mail after the interview. Who knows, you may even be planting a seed for a future job interview.

A word of warning when doing informational interviews: remember that you are getting just one person's perspective. That person may have an extreme bias toward or against the occupation in which they are employed, and it may be reflected in her responses. You should avoid putting too much credence in what just one person has to say. You may want to interview more than one person employed in that occupation in order to get a broader range of opinions. Also keep in mind that while the feedback you get from these individuals is helpful, it should be just one of several factors that go into your ultimate career decision.

A second classification of people as a source of occupational information refers to career planning professionals, also known as career counselors. These are people whose job it is to help you explore, choose, and plan your career. You can find these individuals at your college/university career planning and placement office. They can provide information on the duties and employment qualifications for different jobs. They can also give insight into current occupational trends, which job areas are in demand, salaries, and much more. Their services are usually offered free for students and alumni. There are also private, for-profit, organizations staffed with counselors who can provide similar services, but it is wise to check these out first so you will know what services you will receive for your money.

Occupational Information Publications

One of the largest providers of occupational information is the federal government. The U.S. Department of Labor publishes several books and periodicals that contain an enormous amount of information on occupations and employment in this country. Three of the most comprehensive resource books on occupational information—*Dictionary of Occupational Titles, Occupational Outlook Handbook*, and *Guide for Occupational Exploration*—are all products of the Department of Labor.

The *Dictionary of Occupational Titles* (DOT) lists over 20,000 occupations and classifies them using a nine-digit code which is explained at the beginning of the book. The code, by itself, offers information not only on job titles, but on the nature and working conditions of each title. Additionally, under each title, the DOT offers information on what specifically a worker in that occupation does, what equipment is used, what services are rendered, and other pertinent information that describes the characteristics of that occupation. While the DOT is voluminous and somewhat intimidating at first, it actually is not difficult to use and offers a wealth of information to the career planner.

The *Occupational Outlook Handbook* (OOH) is a favorite tool of many career counselors in aiding others with their career exploration and planning. This reference work is filled with detailed information on occupations covering more than 90% of all jobs and furnishes facts and data on such things as the nature of the work, working conditions, the number of people employed, training and qualifications, the job outlook, and earnings of people employed in each occupation. Additionally the OOH cross-references each career field with others that are similar in nature. This affords the reader the opportunity to learn about similar jobs of which he otherwise may have been unaware. And finally, this resource book provides direction on how to obtain additional information for those who want to learn more about a particular career.

The *Guide for Occupational Exploration* (GOE) is yet another government publication designed to assist career planners. This book groups occupations based on 12 interest areas which are further divided into 66 work groups and 348 subgroups. The GOE uses a six-digit system to classify each occupation. This publication presents information by asking the following five questions of each occupation:

1. What kind of work will you do?
2. What skills and abilities do you need for this kind of work?
3. How do you know if you will like or could learn this type of work?
4. How can you prepare for and enter this kind of work?
5. What else would you consider about these jobs?

The answers given will provide you with a greater understanding of the characteristics of that particular occupational group.

These three publications are some of the better known, most widely used books on occupational information, and you are encouraged to make use of these resources in your career planning. In addition there are many other books available that provide career information. You can learn more by visiting the career resource center at your school or library.

Periodicals

In addition to the books mentioned above, the Department of Labor publishes two periodicals that are worthy of mention—*Occupational Outlook Quarterly* and *Monthly Labor Review*. Both of these publications offer extensive information on careers, trends, demographics, salaries, and numerous other topics pertaining to work. The National Association of Colleges and Employers (NACE) periodically publishes information that can be used in your career planning process. One of their publications, *Job Choices*, offers a great deal of information on a variety of occupations that could prove beneficial in your career planning. As with the books mentioned above, these periodicals can usually be found in your school's library or career resource center.

Exercise 4.2 (at the end of this chapter) presents an excellent way to begin to make use of the printed information sources discussed in this section. By completing an Occupational Analysis, you can gather and organize information from these sources, which will help to further your knowledge of the many different occupations in today's working world. The questions in the Occupational Analysis can be answered by referring to the information sources discussed in this chapter. You may have to go to more than one of the sources to get all of the information you want. As with the informational interview exercise, the insight you gain could prove invaluable in your career decision making and planning.

Other Sources of Occupational Information

While the two main sources of vocational information—people and occupational information publications—are the most widely used, there are a few other ways for you to learn more about career and job characteristics. One of these is career guidance video-tapes. Numerous videos have been produced that present information on occupational characteristics as well as direct the career planner to sources of additional information on careers. Check with a career counselor on your campus; she probably has access to these types of videos or can tell you where to find them.

As technology has continued to advance, computers have become a tool that can be used very effectively in acquiring career information. Software programs are available that provide a variety of career-related information. For instance, information from the *Dictionary of Occupational Titles*, the *Occupational Outlook Handbook*, and other sources have been compiled on computer disk, providing quick, easy access to an enormous amount of information. Examples of these include EZDOT, MicroOOH, and Computerized DOT. As noted in chapter 3, SIGI Plus and Discover are two computer-aided career guidance systems that contain a wealth of occupational information that is quickly and easily accessed. Check to see if any of these programs are available on your campus, and make use of these valuable resources.

Professional associations can almost always provide information about their career fields, usually at no charge. These organizations are in existence to promote their occupational specialty areas, and they will gladly provide information to interested individuals. The *Encycloypedia of Associations* is a publication that contains listings of professional and trade organizations that can be used to find addresses and telephone numbers of specific associations. The Internet can also be used to locate these organizations.

One more source of occupational information, and one that is so obvious you may be surprised that it has not already occurred to you, is direct experience. The knowledge that is gained from actually working in a particular job is an excellent source of information. This can come from full-time jobs you may have held, part-time jobs while in school, internships, co-op positions, as well as volunteer work. Your work experience affords you the opportunity to gather information, firsthand, on the duties, responsibilities, positive and negative aspects, etc., associated with different occupations. This experience will allow you to judge for yourself whether or not you would want to make a career out of a particular occupation.

The problem for college students is that acquiring direct experience is not always feasible. For example, if you would like to learn more about the financial services profession, you can't just walk onto the floor of the New York Stock Exchange and start trading stocks. Most professional jobs like this require several years of education and/or training. It may be otherwise impractical for you to gain direct experience in a given work area due to a lack of time or the unavailability of co-op or internship positions. In such a case, you can still gain on-the-job information by "job shadowing." This activity falls somewhere between a very in-depth informational interview and a very short-term volunteer position. With job shadowing you actually follow someone around, or "shadow" him, while he works. This way you get to see exactly what a person in that particular career field does on a daily basis. Your school may have a job shadowing program where community businesspeople volunteer their time to help students learn more about their field of work. Check with your campus career professionals to see if any such program exists. If not, why not start one? Your career planning and placement office may be able to help you.

SUMMARY

There are many, many sources of occupational information. Relying on information that you acquired years ago does not make for a well-informed career choice. The federal government and private firms are continually producing and updating career information materials. People with knowledge of particular occupations can also provide you with insight that will aid in your choice process. In addition, videotapes, computers, and direct experience can all offer helpful information to those engaged in a career planning program.

EXERCISES AND DISCUSSION QUESTIONS

1. What are your earliest recollections of "work"? Where did they come from? Do you think these early impressions will have any bearing on your ultimate career choice? Why or why not?

2. In comparing the two major sources of career information—people and occupational information publications—what are the advantages of each? What are the disadvantages?

3. Of the jobs (volunteer or paid) you have held, which ones were the most intrinsically rewarding? What aspects of these jobs appealed to you the most? Do these jobs provide any insight into the factors that will contribute to your future career satisfaction? Elaborate.

4. Perform a "scavenger hunt" of occupational information resources available at your school and/or library. Make a list of the books, periodicals, computer programs, and other career information sources you come across in your search. You may even want to make a contest of it with your classmates; see who comes up with the most resources. This exercise is an excellent way to begin to orient yourself to the various sources of career information that are available.

5. After completing the occupational information exercises in this chapter, which careers seem to be the most likely choices right now? What is it specifically that appeals to you about these occupations? Do you need more information on any of these careers? Where can you go to get it?

Exercise 4.1   Informational Interview

Locate someone who is employed in an occupation that is of interest to you. Request either a face-to-face or telephone interview. The purpose of the interview is to acquire information from the individual concerning his or her occupation. This information is to be used to assist you in making your career choice.

Name of person interviewed: _____ Date: _____

Position/JobTitle/Occupation: _____

1. Please describe your duties and responsibilities.
2. What education, degrees, training, licensure, skills, etc., are needed for this job?
3. What do you think the trends in this field are now and in the future?
4. What were the circumstances leading to your employment in this field?
5. What are the opportunities for advancement in this type of job?
6. What are the major advantages of a job like yours?
7. What are the major disadvantages of a job like yours?
8. What do you particularly like about your job?
9. What do you particularly dislike about your job?
10. What is the most important advice you could give me as I consider a job similar to yours as a possible career?

Interpretation

After completing this interview, what is your level of interest in this occupation? _____

_____

Does it warrant further investigation as a possible career? _____

_____

Are there any other information sources you should seek out? If so, list them. _____

_____

Exercise 4.2   Occupational Analysis

Choose an occupation that you would like to learn more about. Using as many of the information sources listed in this chapter as are necessary, find answers to the questions below. Locate any additional information that you deem important as you consider this occupation as a potential career.

Occupation Title:_____

1. What are the characteristics of the nature of this occupation?
2. What is the outlook for employment in this occupation over the next 5–10 years?
3. What education, training, and/or other qualifications are needed for entry into this field?
4. What is the typical entry-level salary for people in this occupation? What is the average salary? Upper range?
5. What are the typical working hours for someone employed in this profession?
6. Identify two or three occupations that are similar to this one.
7. Where can you find additional information on this occupation?

Interpretation

After completing this analysis, what is your level of interest in this occupation? _____

_____

Does it seem to be consistent with your values, interests, abilities, and personal traits? Why or why not? _____

_____

Does it warrant further investigation as a possible career? _____

_____

Are there any other informational sources you should seek out? If so, list them. _____

_____

Career Decision Making
and Goal Setting

After completing this chapter you should understand

- *The dynamics of the decision-making process*
- *Which criteria are important in making a well-reasoned career choice*
- *The importance of goal setting in the career planning process*
- *What guidelines should be used in setting career goals*
- *The difference between long-term and short-term goals and the relationship of each to career objectives*

INTRODUCTION

We have now completed our discussion of the two preliminary phases of the career guidance and decision-making stage (Figure 5.1). By satisfactorily addressing the concepts in these phases, you should have gained a deeper understanding of yourself, as well as a basic knowledge of various occupations. Now comes the point in the career planning process that, for many, proves to be the most difficult part—actually making a career choice. For some, one career path will stand out above the rest as the best option. For others, there may be two, three, or more work groups that all seem appealing and appropriate for their capabilities. If you find that you have completed the first two phases and are still undecided, don't panic. This is quite normal, and there are methods for evaluating and "fine tuning" your decision making.

INFLUENCES ON CAREER DECISION MAKING

Before we take a look at the criteria used in evaluating career options and how you can effectively fine tune and narrow your choices, it is helpful to gain an understanding of the factors that impact career decision making. In other words, what circumstances occur in people's lives that influence their ultimate career choice? Two of the major determinants of occupational choice are (1) genetic endowment and special abilities—that which fate has dealt each individual—and (2) cultural/environmental conditions and events (Mitchell, Jones, & Krumboltz, 1979).

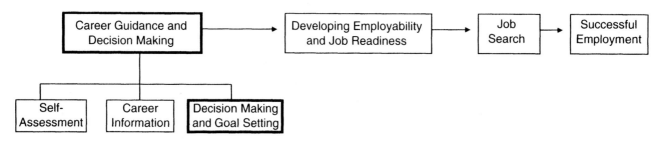

FIGURE 5.1
The Decision-Making and Goal-Setting Phase

Genetic endowments are inherited traits that people are born with and include characteristics such as gender, physical appearance, physical ability, and creative/artistic talent. Each of us has special abilities that we are born with and certain areas in which we are lacking. Obviously, these factors will play a big role in the career options that are available to each of us.

The cultural/environmental conditions that influence the choice process include factors as broad ranging as occupational supply and demand, jobs held by our parents and other family members, and those jobs that we see on television and in films. Of course, the working conditions and income potential of different jobs are also choice factors.

Expanding the concept of career decision-making influences, it is apparent that our choices are affected by both fate and our own efforts. The continuum in Figure 5.2 represents our opportunity to make choices. The left side of the continuum represents the role that fate plays in determining what career choice options we will have by endowing us with unique abilities, limitations, and other factors over which we have little or no control. The inherited traits listed above provide some examples of this.

Chance occurrence is another act of fate that can influence decision making. Meeting someone by happenstance who ultimately influences your career choice is not uncommon. A significant percentage of people today are in their field of work simply because they met someone who guided them into a career field. A business executive, for example, after meeting an exceptionally bright individual at a party might say: "We are always looking for sharp people like you. Have you ever thought about the public relations field?" Further exploration and discussions may land that person in a new career in public relations. No real career planning took place that resulted in him ending up in the PR field, it just happened. Some may call this luck, or just being in the right place at the right time. Regardless of the terminology applied to it, chance obviously plays a role in determining the career choice of some.

Represented at the other end of the continuum, the deterministic side, is our ability to make choices that enable us to take control of our future and accomplish our objectives. While we can never escape fate, we do have the capacity to exercise responsibility and manipulate our circumstances to effect positive results from our career choices. So regardless of what fate deals us, or how much "luck" we have, or don't have, we ultimately control the direction of our lives by our choices.

Let's take a closer look at the decision-making process and how we can use it to maximize the control we have over our own destiny.

FIGURE 5.2
Decision-Making
Opportunities

Fate   Deterministic

Less control   More control

THE DECISION-MAKING PROCESS

 What criteria should you use in making a career choice?

Having adequately studied the self-assessment aspects and the career information factors pertinent to career decision making, you are now faced with actually making a career choice. What criteria should you use in making your decision? While there are several factors you should consider, ultimately there is one fundamental rule on which you should base your decision: *Choose a career about which you are passionate.* There is probably no better formula for ensuring career satisfaction and success. By opting for work that you thoroughly enjoy, that you delight in and look forward to, you have established a foundation for later career happiness.

Choosing a career that integrates into your work the things that you naturally enjoy and find engaging will have obvious consequences. Imagine how wonderful it would be to have a job that truly excites you; one that you look forward to each day. The enthusiasm and drive you have for this kind of work can help you achieve the success and recognition that results in a happy, rewarding career.

> **Fundamental rule for career decision making:**
>
> Choose a career about which you are passionate.

Ignoring this fundamental rule and choosing a career based merely on income possibilities, or the expectations of family and friends, can cause you to enter a career that will never prove to be personally rewarding. You may find yourself, as many do, in a job that you hate, working only because you cannot afford to quit, and dreading going to work each day. You should avoid this plight at all costs. By choosing a career you believe you would truly enjoy, you can help ensure that you do not fall into the same predicament as those workers who wish they were doing something else.

This concept of choosing something that you enjoy doing can be extended to off-the-job activities as well. Be sure to factor into your career decision-making process the extent to which your chosen occupation would allow you to engage in hobbies and other enjoyable nonwork pursuits. For example, if you love to go hiking and camping on weekends, choosing an occupation that requires a substantial amount of weekend work can cause you to resent your job after a short time. A job that forces you to be away from home and family for extended periods of time—as is sometimes the case with military personnel and outside sales representatives—can also result in personal and career dissatisfaction for those who put a premium on family life. Just as a fulfilling job can help lead to a happy personal life, pursuing hobbies and interests off the job can take some of the routineness out of your weekly schedule, add a sense of balance, and result in more job satisfaction. By "recharging your batteries" with fun and relaxation, you can return to work refreshed, with renewed vigor and enthusiasm.

EVALUATIVE CRITERIA IN DECISION MAKING

Choosing an occupation in which you have a high degree of interest is, of course, important. But there are other factors that need to be considered in your decision-making process. You should evaluate each of your options with respect to those factors that will play the biggest role in determining your level of career satisfaction. This can be done most effectively by making a list of factors that are important to you in your job and career. This list should include both *internal* and *external* factors. Internal factors are those elements that come from within you. Looking back to the exercises in chapter 3 will give you insight into some of the intrinsic factors that should be used as evaluative criteria; specifically your interests, values, abilities, and traits.

The external factors are those areas that are not from within you, but rather are the environmental circumstances inherent in the occupation. Future employment demand, amount of education needed, and average starting salary for a given occupation are examples of this type of factor.

Exercise 5.1, Decision-Making Grid (at the end of this chapter), provides a rating system whereby you can evaluate and compare two or more career alternatives to see how they stack up against each other. This exercise focuses largely on the self-assessment characteristics outlined in chapter 3, with particular emphasis on evaluating career options with respect to one's values. Experts agree that the best-made career decisions are those that follow a values-guided search (Krumboltz, Rude, Mitchell, Hamel, & Kinnier, 1982); hence this exercise emphasizes the importance of linking one's values to career options. Be aware that this exercise should be used only to help you better organize information to facilitate the decision-making process, not to actually make your choice for you.

One more important point about decision making. While it is perfectly acceptable to seek other's advice and opinions, remember that the ultimate choice is yours, and yours alone. Nobody can decide for you, nor should you let them. Along these lines, Gordon Porter Miller writes:

> Far too often, people tend to lay out alternatives for you. As a result, you may focus on only those alternatives. But you should always keep in mind that there may be other alternatives that haven't been mentioned by anyone. Also, you are bringing what is uniquely you to the situation, so that an alternative that may be best for most people may not be best for you (as cited in Borchard, Kelly, & Weaver, 1992, p. 129).

Following the guidelines outlined in this first stage of the career development model will prepare you well for making this decision. Remember the fundamental rule—choose an occupation about which you are passionate—and choose wisely.

INTEGRATED CAREERS

Something to keep in mind when making an occupational choice is the idea of *integrated careers*. If you find yourself debating between two equally attractive occupations, consider that it may be possible for you to incorporate both of them into your career choice. You may be able to combine elements of each of these occupational interests into a single line of work. Taking a creative approach may enable you to "custom fit" what you want into a career. For example, if in your career exploration you discovered that you are interested in both the business and education fields, you may want to double major in these areas and pursue a career in educational product sales (Figure 5.3). A job as a marketing representative for a textbook publishing firm would allow you to work in the education field as well as the business field. Similarly, if journalism and health care both seem like viable career options, how about writing or editing for a medical journal? It would probably take some time to acquire the requisite training and experience, but it could be a workable goal. The possibilities for combining elements of different occupational interest areas into a career are endless.

FIGURE 5.3
Integrated Careers

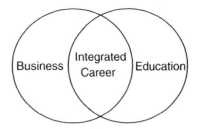

Even if you choose one occupation, it may still be possible for you to pursue another area on the side. Many people have achieved fame and fortune by beginning an enterprise as a sideline to their "real" job. So allow yourself to be creative in your choice process. Do not limit your scope of possibilities to only a single occupation.

IMPEDIMENTS TO THE CAREER CHOICE PROCESS

A common fallacy and a source of fear for many who are in the career decision-making mode is their idea that once they make their choice, there is no going back; they see their decision as permanent. This causes them to postpone the decision until they feel more confident about their choice. However, the fear of being "stuck" forever with their choice is almost always unfounded. Making a choice of careers is not a one-time event. As was pointed out in chapter 1, it is part of an ongoing developmental process. Statistics show that the typical American worker will be employed in at least three distinctly different occupations over the course of a career. Therefore, it is important for you to understand that when you make your decision to enter a certain line of work, you are not necessarily making a choice that you will have to live with forever. Realizing this can help to take the fear and finality out of your decision, thereby facilitating the choice process.

A second impediment to the decision-making process is a lack of information. As with any major decision, the more you know, the better prepared you will be to make the best choice. Much of the fear surrounding occupational choice can be lessened by successfully completing the self-assessment and career information phases of the career guidance and decision-making stage. Those people who have not addressed these initial steps may feel uninformed and experience apprehension, even to the point of refusing to decide. To avoid this problem it is imperative that you feel that you have "covered all the bases" in your exploratory journey. The more information you acquire, the more comfortable you will be about making such an important decision and the smoother the process will be. Recalling Disraeli's quote from chapter 1 concerning successful people, if you have obtained the best information about yourself and the world of work, you will be in an excellent position to make a well-reasoned choice.

In addition to a lack of information, inaccurate information can also prevent you from making a good career choice. For example, if you had heard two years ago that a certain occupation was not expected to grow much and would, therefore, not be a good career choice, you could be making a mistake by assuming that the same is true today. It could be that today that career field is in big demand and expected to grow. Take steps to ensure that the information you have acquired is accurate and up to date.

Apathy can also be a barrier to overcome in the career decision-making process. Some may adopt an attitude of "I'm not going to worry about choosing a career, I'll just take whatever occupation comes my way." Such an attitude can result in ill-conceived choices and a lot of discontent.

If you find yourself about to enter the decision-making stage, and you still have a feeling of unpreparedness, you may need to reenter one of the first two stages of the career development model and complete or possibly reevaluate the tasks in that phase. Did you acquire all of the necessary information? Is there something else you need to understand or do before you can make a well-informed career choice? You may find that by read-dressing these phases you can fill in the gaps of the missing information, allowing you to feel more prepared to make a decision. The career development model is designed to enable you to choose with confidence.

GOAL SETTING

People with goals succeed because they know where they are going.

Earl Nightingale

After having made a career choice, it is important for you to begin to identify some career and personal goals. Pertinent questions will need to be addressed: Where do you want to be in five years? Ten years? Twenty years? What steps can you take to ensure achievement of these goals? Setting goals offers you the opportunity to create a plan for success and gives direction and purpose to the career you have chosen. Having no goals is a prescription for failure. Without the direction and purpose provided by goals it is extremely difficult to excel. A person without goals is leaving his success to happenstance, and accidental success is much more rare than that which has been planned.

Goal-Setting Guidelines

There are a few guidelines to consider when goal setting that help to make your goals more clear. The best goals are those that are (1) specific, (2) planned, (3) achievable, (4) controllable, and (5) written (Figure 5.4). Let's take a look at each of these factors and how you can incorporate them into your goals.

Specific. Your goals should be specific enough so that there is no ambiguity in knowing exactly what it is that you want from a given goal. Saying "I want to be employed in some sort of job that helps people" is so broad as to include thousands of possibilities, from gas-station attendant to neurosurgeon. On the other hand, a goal of working as "a social worker helping underprivileged children" is specific and clearly identifies an occupational objective. Without specificity, attainment of a goal becomes open for debate. In other words, you will have a difficult time determining whether or not you have actually reached your goal. Your goals should be explicit enough so that you know exactly what you want to achieve.

FIGURE 5.4
Goal-Setting Guidelines

Good Goals Are
Specific
Planned
Achievable
Controllable
Written

Similarly, good goals are always measurable, meaning that you should be able to tell exactly when that goal has been achieved. If you were to set one of your goals as "I want to be wealthy," what is it that defines "wealthy"? A net worth of $100,000? $200,000? $1,000,000? Without some sort of quantitative measure, you will not know if or when you achieve your goal.

A timetable may also be needed in setting some of your goals. A goal to own your own advertising agency before you are 35 puts a time limit on when you plan to achieve that objective. While placing time limits on your goals may seem to be limiting your chances for success, actually just the opposite is true. Time constraints have the effect of making people face up to their self-imposed deadlines, and by establishing a time frame, one is more likely to take the steps necessary to reach a goal. To illustrate this, think back to the times when you have had a project or assignment that you had put off until the last minute. As the deadline approached, you worked doubly hard in order to get the work done. The same principle applies to your career goals. By creating a timetable for completion of a goal, you are more likely to take steps now to make sure that you beat the deadline. Without a deadline, it is easy to adopt an attitude of "What's the rush, I've got plenty of time," and end up postponing any work toward your goal.

Planned.   All of this leads us directly into another important aspect of effective goal setting—planning. It is not enough to merely decide what your goals are, you need to create a plan to achieve them. Developing a plan of action for goal attainment gives you a road map, guiding you to your career and personal objectives. Most people find it easier to work toward a goal if they look at it in terms of smaller, easier-to-accomplish objectives, rather than as one big step. Therefore it is desirable in goal setting to include both long-term and short-term, or interim, goals. Long-term goals are more substantial, harder-to-achieve objectives which usually require the fulfillment of one or more interim goals. For example, the goal of becoming a corporate vice president for a Fortune 500 firm by the age of 40 may be your long-term goal. An interim goal, then, may be to move into a management position within two years, or it could be to acquire an MBA which will open more doors as you move up the corporate ladder. The sense of accomplishment enjoyed upon completion of each interim step can motivate you to work toward the next. By undertaking, and achieving, these intermediate steps, the attainment of your ultimate goal becomes much easier.

As you can see from the simplified example presented in Figure 5.5, each of the steps in the plan to become a pediatrician is an accomplishment in and of itself. The satisfaction of completing each of the steps, or interim goals, can provide the impetus for continuing the journey. Without the steps, the goal looks like one big unattainable task. This type of planning can make the difference between a successful career and failure.

A vital aspect of goal attainment, then, is designing a plan to get what you want and working diligently on that plan. Failing to plan or relying solely on fate to get you to your career goals is a lot like looking in a showroom window, wishing for that shiny new convertible. If you merely admire it and hope that you get one someday, it *could* happen. On the other hand, if you create and implement a plan to work hard, save a certain amount of money each month, and buy it after you have acquired the needed funds, it is almost a *certainty* that you will own it. Creating a plan and sticking to it is an important guideline to remember when setting goals.

Achievable.   Another characteristic of a good goal is that it is achievable. Will Rogers said that people should set their goals high enough that they have to work hard for them, but not so high as to be out of reach. If you do set unrealistically high goals, you could be setting yourself up for a lifetime of frustration because you will seldom achieve that which you set out to do. Setting a goal to make a million dollars your first year out of college meets the criteria of being specific and measurable, but it is unrealistic. Make your goals be something that you feel as though you have a good chance of obtaining,

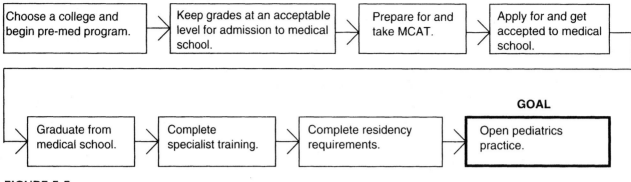

FIGURE 5.5
Goal Planning Chart

but only with a diligent effort. Finding a balance between setting high goals and realistic ones is an important part of the goal-setting process.

Controllable.   In deciding your future goals, you should include only those factors over which you have control. If your goal is to reach financial independence through winning a lottery, or a similar act of fate or luck, you have given away control of your goals. Hoping that your dream job will fall into your lap is similarly relinquishing control. Your goals should never be left to chance. Make sure that when you actually begin to set your career and personal goals that you make your plans based on what *you* can accomplish through *your* efforts, not what might happen as a consequence of luck or similar uncontrollable factors.

Written.   Finally, your goals should be written down on paper and placed somewhere easily accessible and noticeable. The reason for this is quite simple: goals that are written are a lot more likely to be achieved than those that are not. By writing your goals on paper you have created a permanent record of what you want to accomplish, and this record acts as a constant reminder to you of what you are working toward. Without this reminder it is easy to lose sight of your goals and neglect your plans. Along with your goals include the step-by-step plan you have created to accomplish each goal. Keep this "goal sheet" in a safe place and take it out regularly to see where you are and to check off the interim goals as each is accomplished. By doing this you keep your goals fresh in your mind and increase the likelihood of achieving all of your goals.

Flexible Goals

One overriding factor to keep in mind when you are establishing career goals is that they may change over time. While at first glance this may seem to be inconsistent with the notion of being dedicated to your goals, it really is not. As people mature their interests, values, abilities, and needs may change. The things that are important to you when you are a 19-year-old college student may not seem so important when you reach 30. This change is a natural consequence of the human maturation process and is to be expected. As a consequence, your goals may need to be reevaluated and restructured. Inflexibility in adhering to outdated objectives can cause you to pursue old dreams that are no longer desirable. Therefore, allowing for flexibility in changing your goals is not only acceptable, it is encouraged.

Career Navigation

The term "career navigation" (Fisher, 1984) addresses this concept of flexibility and stresses the need for continual reassessment of where you are and where you want to go. An appropriate analogy is that of an oceangoing vessel. Just as the captain of a ship has to navigate his vessel in order to arrive at the desired destination, the person who wants to achieve career goals will likewise engage in a form of navigation. While plotting a course is necessary for both of these individuals, the inevitable changes in their journeys will force them to adjust their plans. The ship captain may find himself heading into a storm, forcing him to modify his travel route. Similarly, a worker may find herself "blown off course" by any number of circumstances. A layoff, promotion, transfer, or career change may force her to realign her goals. What was once a feasible goal may no longer be so, and conversely, an opportunity that once seemed out of reach, may now be very attainable. Throughout your career you will occasionally be faced with opportunities, events, and decisions; the ability to change, or navigate, is vital to a successful career. Finding a balance between the determination to achieve your goals and the flexibility to adjust them when necessary is the surest way to reach the pinnacle of success in your career.

Unfortunately there is no blueprint to follow that will show you how to navigate your career. Everybody is different, and as such they will handle life's challenges differently. What may be best for someone else may not be best for you. So as you reach turning points and crossroads in your career and personal life, you will need to choose what you believe are the best alternatives for you, navigating your way to career and personal success. The important lesson here is that you are the master of your own destiny and the navigational process is just beginning when you make your career choice. In the words of Ben Sweetland, "Success is a journey, not a destination."

To help you with your goal setting and planning, complete Exercise 5.2, appropriately titled Career Goal Setting and Planning (at the end of this chapter). This exercise will take your through the process of deciding what you want from your career and guide you in creating a plan for success. Even if you have not absolutely decided on a career choice, you can still practice your goal-setting and planning skills by choosing a tentative career and setting goals and plans based on that choice. Later, after you have made your career decision, you can return to this exercise and design your true career goals and plans.

SUMMARY

Making a career choice is a process that involves gathering, analyzing, and integrating information so as to make a thoughtful, well-informed decision. The goal is to find a strong match between the internal factors that the individual brings to the workplace and the external characteristics associated with potential occupations. Although several factors should be figured into the decision, such as consistency with one's abilities, traits, and values, ultimately there is one fundamental rule that should not be violated when making a career choice: choose an occupation about which you are passionate. By doing so, the motivation and drive needed for career success comes naturally.

There are many obstacles that can foul up the choice process. The fear of making a long-term commitment, a lack of information or inaccurate information, and even apathy can wreak havoc on the decision-making process. By following the guidelines offered by the career development model, many of the impediments to career choice can be overcome.

In addition to making a career choice, it is important for everyone involved in a career planning program to set goals and create plans to achieve them. Having no goals is a sure way to inhibit career success. And actually, without goals, there can be no success because it is goals that create the benchmark which determines your success. When developing career goals, there are guidelines one should keep in mind. Good goals are specific, planned, achievable, controllable, and written. Since career satisfaction is partially determined by factors that cannot be predicted or controlled by the decider (Krumboltz et al., 1982), it is necessary to build a degree of flexibility into one's goals. Because of changes in the individual or changes in the job, or both, what was once important may become less so with time. Thus the term "career navigation" was coined, stressing the need for continual reassessment of where one is in their career development process.

EXERCISES AND DISCUSSION QUESTIONS

1. Make a list of the 10 most important factors in choosing your career. Which one(s) are you absolutely unwilling to sacrifice? Why? Which ones are negotiable? Why?

2. With what you know about yourself today, and with the information that you currently have on various occupations, describe your ideal job. Include information on what you would be doing, where you would live, and also noncareer information such as your leisure activities, etc.

3. If all jobs paid the same after you graduate from college, regardless of the degree you obtained or the career field you entered, what occupation would you choose? Is this different from your answer in question 2? If so, why the change?

4. Of the impediments to career choice mentioned in this chapter, which ones, if any, do you think you will have to overcome? Are there any others that you feel you will have to face? What steps can you take to help you overcome these barriers?

5. Elaborate on the goals that you have for yourself at this point in your career development. List either career or personal goals. Why are these things important to you? Use these goals to complete Exercise 5.2.

Exercise 5.1   Decision-Making Grid

Having successfully completed the self-assessment and career information phases, most people will have narrowed their search to just a few options. This exercise will help to further refine the decision-making process.

1. Place the title of each occupational field that you are still considering in the box under each option.
2. Using the information compiled in Exercises 3.1–3.5 as a guide, rate each of the career options you have chosen as to the degree to which you believe it relates to the decisional criteria listed. Using the rating scale provided will enable you to evaluate how well suited you believe each career option would be to those factors that are important to you.

Section One: Abilities, Personality Traits, and Interests Scale

When evaluating each of the first three decisional criteria, ask yourself "How well does this career suit my abilities? Personal traits? Interests?"

1	2	3	4	5
Not Well Suited		Somewhat Suited		Very Well Suited

Example:

Decisional Criteria	Option 1 Accountant	Option 2 Doctor	Option 3 Lawyer	Option 4
Abilities	3	2	3	
Personality Traits	4	5	4	
Interests	5	3	5	
Total for Section One	12	10	12	

Decisional Criteria	Option 1	Option 2	Option 3	Option 4
Abilities				
Personality Traits				
Interests				
Total for Section One				

Section Two: Work Values Scale

When evaluating the work values listed below, use the given scale and ask yourself, "What is the probability that this career will allow me to achieve, or satisfy, this value?" If one of the values listed is not important to you in making a career choice, give a rating of zero across the board for that value.

1	2	3	4	5
Low Probability		Moderate Probability		High Probability

Work Values	Option 1	Option 2	Option 3	Option 4
Advancement				
High income				
Challenging				
Helping others				
Prestige				
Public contact				
Security				
Location				
Flexible hours				
Influencing people				
Making decisions				
Independence				
Creativity				
Excitement				
Other criteria:				
Total for Section Two				
Total for Section One				
TOTAL (add both sections)				

Interpretation

Having evaluated your top career options, which one seems most likely to be your first choice? _____

_____

What will entrance into this field require you to do? Are you willing to put forth the time and effort needed to become successfully employed in this occupation? _____

_____

Is there any additional information that you need before you make a career choice? If so, where can you get this information? _____

_____

Exercise 5.2   Career Goal Setting and Planning

After making a career choice, it is important to begin to set goals and develop plans. By asking yourself "What do I want to accomplish?" you will begin to identify long term and interim goals (you may want to reread the section in this chapter on planning, page 55, to clarify the difference between these).

After analyzing what you want to accomplish, list your goals below, then list the steps you will need to take to achieve each one. There are no minimum or maximum number of steps; it depends on the goal and what you feel is appropriate in reaching it.

Use this system throughout your career as you "navigate" your way to continued successful employment.

Goal #1 _____   Will achieve by _____
                                                            date

    Step 1 _____   Will achieve by _____

    Step 2 _____   Will achieve by _____

    Step 3 _____   Will achieve by _____

    Step 4 _____   Will achieve by _____

    Step 5 _____   Will achieve by _____

    Step 6 _____   Will achieve by _____

    Step 7 _____   Will achieve by _____

    Step 8 _____   Will achieve by _____

Add additional steps as needed.

Goal #2 _____   Will achieve by _____
                                                            date

    Step 1 _____   Will achieve by _____

    Step 2 _____   Will achieve by _____

    Step 3 _____   Will achieve by _____

    Step 4 _____   Will achieve by _____

    Step 5 _____   Will achieve by _____

    Step 6 _____   Will achieve by _____

    Step 7 _____   Will achieve by _____

    Step 8 _____   Will achieve by _____

Add additional steps as needed.

Goal #3 _____   Will achieve by _____
                                                            date

    Step 1 _____   Will achieve by _____

    Step 2 _____   Will achieve by _____

    Step 3 _____   Will achieve by _____

    Step 4 _____   Will achieve by _____

    Step 5 _____   Will achieve by _____

    Step 6 _____   Will achieve by _____

    Step 7 _____   Will achieve by _____

    Step 8 _____   Will achieve by _____

Add additional steps as needed.

6

Functional Qualities

After completing this chapter you should understand

- *What the general qualities employers look for in hiring their personnel are*
- *How your level of knowledge in your occupational field affects your degree of marketability*
- *What the difference is between job-specific and transferable skills and the part each plays in your career success*
- *How your work experience affects your degree of marketability*

INTRODUCTION TO STAGE 2: DEVELOPING EMPLOYABILITY AND JOB READINESS

Having successfully completed each of the three components of the career guidance and decision-making stage, you should have made a decision concerning the type of work you want to do and are now ready to move to the next step in the model (Figure 6.1). In this stage, developing employability and job readiness, your task is to develop a plan to make yourself marketable and appealing to prospective employers. This includes acquiring the education and skills that employers want in their employees, as well as learning how to write a good resume and develop strong interviewing skills. Look at this stage in these terms: Imagine that at the time you make your career choice, you are given a checklist (Figure 6.2) that itemizes all of the credentials you will need in order to become "successfully employed." Some of the items on your checklist are mandatory—absolutely necessary for employment—while others are merely helpful, but not required. Every time you achieve, or acquire, one of these employability factors, you can check it off your list. The more items on your list that are checked off, the more marketable and employable you become, thereby

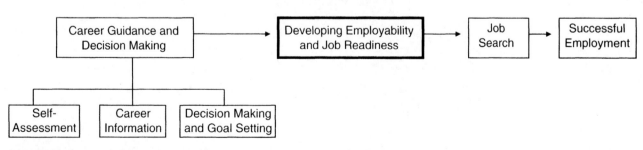

FIGURE 6.1
Developing Employability and Job Readiness

FIGURE 6.2
Employability Checklist

```
┌─────────────────────────────────┐
│      Employability Checklist      │
│   ☐ _____           │
│   ☐ _____           │
│   ☐ _____           │
│   ☐ _____           │
│   ☐ _____           │
│   ☐ _____           │
└─────────────────────────────────┘
```

increasing the likelihood that you will be offered the job that you want. For example, if you have decided on civil engineering as your career choice, a few of the items on your employability checklist might include

- Obtain a degree in civil engineering
- Maintain a 3.0/4.0 grade point average
- Join campus engineering organizations
- Acquire an internship or co-op position with a reputable firm

The whole idea behind "developing your employability" is to find out which attributes and qualifications employers in your career field look for when hiring and work toward acquiring as many of them as possible. A discussion of these "functional qualities" is provided later in this chapter.

Other aspects of developing employability and job readiness that are discussed in chapters 7–9 are resume writing, employment correspondence, and interviewing skills. It is imperative that you learn how to present yourself and your qualifications to prospective employers in a way that demonstrates how you can be of benefit to them. The ability to market yourself effectively is an essential element of your career development.

FUNCTIONAL QUALITIES

From our discussion in chapter 2, it is obvious that as we head into the 21st century the structure of the workplace will continue to change. The 1980s and 1990s have seen a trend in both business and government toward downsizing. This new workplace is characterized by fewer employees, lower personnel costs, higher productivity, improved quality, and better customer service. The expectation is that this trend toward streamlining and the elimination of management layers within organizations will continue. All of this restructuring has resulted in what has been called the "high-performance workplace," described as "extraordinarily capable people, working in teams, equipped with proper technology, focused on satisfying the customer and improving work processes" (White, 1994). This stage of the career development model forces you to examine the changing work environment and gain an understanding of what you must do in order to be competitive.

 What qualities do employers look for when hiring their employees?

In chapter 3 we examined the need for self-assessment in career guidance and decision making. The information that you acquired helped you gain insight into the quali-

FIGURE 6.3
Functional Qualities

> **Functional Qualities**
> - Knowledge
> - Skills
> - Experience

ties you possess that may prove helpful in choosing a career. Now it is time to turn your attention to a similar group of characteristics—your "functional qualities," which are the (1) knowledge, (2) skills, and (3) experience you possess regarding your career field (Figure 6.3). These are the critical elements on which you will be evaluated during interviews, and they play a major role in determining how marketable you are. Potential employers want to know what level of knowledge you have in your occupational area, what degree of skills you possess (this includes job-specific as well as transferable skills, discussed later), and how much related experience you have. Employers are well aware of the consequences of making a poor choice in the hiring process. The loss of time, money, and resources that goes into hiring and training a worker can quickly run into tens of thousands of dollars. As a result, organizations look for just the right person before making a job offer. Therefore it is helpful to take steps to become as employable as possible.

Conducting an evaluation of your functional qualities is somewhat similar to the self-assessment you performed in the first stage of the career development model; however, an important distinction needs to be made between these two stages. In chapter 3 you were assessing your interests, abilities, values, and personality traits to help you in making a career choice. Now, with functional qualities, you are evaluating yourself from another perspective—that of an employer. Well before you actually begin employment interviewing, you should do an analysis of how you rate in each of the functional quality areas and begin making a plan to strengthen your overall level of employability. We will now take a closer look at the functional qualities and the components that make up each.

Knowledge

Knowledge refers to the level of understanding that you have in your occupational area. When interviewing, prospective employers want to know how much you know about the area in which you will be employed. Typically your knowledge is acquired through education, on-the-job training, or both. From an employer's perspective, the more you know, the less training you will require and the more you will be able to contribute to the organization. They will be concerned with how relevant your educational background is to what will be needed on the job. They want to know if you will be able to translate your school work into productive functions on the job. It is up to you to demonstrate that you have the appropriate knowledge and are competent to handle the responsibilities of the position for which you are applying.

Also, any potential employer will be interested in your ability and desire to add to your pool of knowledge by participating in continuing education and training. Since we live in such a dynamic period of workplace change, the knowledge that you currently possess can easily become outdated in a short period of time. This is especially true with respect to technological advancements that impact the way work is performed, and which are in a never-ending state of change. Continually adding to your knowledge is a requirement in order to keep pace with the current trends in your field. Your ability to do so will, in part, determine your level of employability.

Skills

There is a strong link between the functional qualities of knowledge and skills. Skills represent your ability to apply the knowledge that you have acquired to a specific job. In making plans to develop your employability rating, it is important to consider *job-specific skills* as well as *transferable skills*. Job-specific skills are those that are typically used only within a single occupational field. Drafting, for example, is almost exclusively used by people in engineering-related fields. Labor-related jobs, in particular, require acquisition of job-specific skills. Quite often these skills are developed through on-the-job training and only become more refined through experience.

Significantly more important for your long-term career success are transferable skills, which are much more broad and can be used in many different jobs and careers. Examples of these types of skills include writing, problem solving, critical thinking, management, and interpersonal skills. Not surprisingly, many of these skills can be found in the SCANS report (see chapter 2), which describes the skills necessary for success in the workplace of today.

The necessity of obtaining these skills in order to increase one's employability is illustrated in a survey published in *Training* magazine (Gordon, 1994). In the survey, Olsten Corporation, a temporary-help firm based in New York City, asked companies about their workers' skill needs and what steps the companies were taking to ensure that their employees have the necessary skills to adequately perform their job duties. The results are very interesting.

Fifty-one percent of the organizations surveyed reported that their employees' skills were inadequate, up from 34% the previous year. To help in overcoming the skills gap, companies are trying to hire more qualified workers. More than half indicated that they have improved their screening processes. Since companies are placing more emphasis on finding workers with the right skills, making sure that you have these skills will help keep you from becoming "screened out" in the hiring process.

We will now take a closer look at the SCANS report skills. Remember, these are the skills that employers have identified as being required in their employees, and you are encouraged to begin evaluating yourself as to your level of proficiency in these areas, and if necessary, make plans for improvement.

SCANS Report Skills. As the nature of the workplace continues to change, the skills necessary in order to compete for jobs also continue to evolve. Few jobs will continue to exist that allow workers to be trained once to do a job and then rely on that training for the rest of their career. The fact that workers now regularly shift from job to job and from one career field to another has caused a shift toward emphasizing the development of transferable skills rather than job-specific skills. This is not to say that job-specific skills are no longer important, but rather it illustrates that transferable skills are becoming increasingly more essential in order to keep pace with the changes in the way work is performed.

In identifying and classifying the skills required for solid job performance in today's workplace, the SCANS report divides skills into two categories: competencies and foundations. *Competencies* are the specific abilities necessary for worker success; *foundation skills*, as the name implies, are the underlying, more basic abilities that are used in performing the competencies. For example, the abilities to read and write are both foundation skills and are needed to interpret and communicate information, which are competencies. Take time to become familiar with the information presented in Table 6.1, which profiles each of the competencies and foundations. These are the skills that are necessary for success in today's workplace. By examining the information presented, you can begin to assess where you are weak and develop plans to acquire the skills you believe will most help you in your chosen profession. If you are uncertain as to which skills are most desired by employers in your chosen field, a return to the career information phase (chapter 4) may be in order. An appointment with a career counselor, informational interviewing (Exercise 4.1), or an occupational analysis (Exercise 4.2) can provide you with this type of information.

TABLE 6.1
Workplace Skills

	SCANS Competencies
RESOURCES	
Allocates time	Selects relevant, goal-related activities, ranks them in order of importance, allocates time to activities, and understands, prepares, and follows schedules.
Allocates money	Uses or prepares budgets, including making cost and revenue forecasts, keeps detailed records to track budget performance, and makes appropriate adjustments.
Allocates material and facility resources	Acquires, stores, and distributes materials, supplies, parts, equipment, space, or final products in order to make the best use of them.
Allocates human resources	Assesses knowledge and skills and distributes work accordingly, evaluates performance and provides feedback.
INFORMATION	
Acquires and evaluates information	Identifies need for data, obtains them from existing sources or creates them, and evaluates their relevance and accuracy.
Organizes and maintains information	Organizes, processes, and maintains written or computerized records and other forms of information in a systematic fashion.
Interprets and communicates information	Selects and analyzes information and communicates the results to others using oral, written, graphic, pictorial, or multimedia methods.
Uses computers to process information	Employs computers to acquire, organize, analyze, and communicate information.
INTERPERSONAL	
Participates as a member of a team	Works cooperatively with others and contributes to group with ideas, suggestions, and effort.
Teaches others	Helps others learn.
Serves clients/customers	Works and communicates with clients and customers to satisfy their expectations.
Exercises leadership	Communicates thoughts, feelings, and ideas to justify a position, encourages, persuades, convinces, or otherwise motivates an individual or groups, including responsibly challenging existing procedures, policies, or authority.
Negotiates to arrive at a decision	Works toward an agreement that may involve exchanging specific resources or resolving divergent interests.
Works with cultural diversity	Works well with men and women and with a variety of ethnic, social, or educational backgrounds.
SYSTEMS	
Understands systems	Knows how social, organizational, and technological systems work and operates effectively within them.
Monitors and corrects performance	Distinguishes trends, predicts impact of actions on system operations, diagnoses deviations in the function of a system/organization, and takes necessary action to correct performance.
Improves and designs systems	Makes suggestions to modify existing systems to improve products or services, and develops new or alternative systems.

(continued on next page)

TABLE 6.1
(continued)

	SCANS Competencies
TECHNOLOGY	
Selects technology	Judges which set of procedures, tools, or machines, including computers and their programs, will produce the desired results.
Applies technology to task	Understands the overall intent and the proper procedures for setting up and operating machines, including computers and their programming systems.
Maintains and troubleshoots technology	Prevents, identifies, or solves problems in machines, computers, and other technologies.

	SCANS Foundation Skills
BASIC SKILLS	
Reading	Locates, understands, and interprets written information in prose and documents—including manuals, graphs, and schedules—to perform tasks; learns from text by determining the main idea or essential message; identifies relevant details, facts, and specifications; infers or locates the meaning of unknown or technical vocabulary; judges the accuracy, appropriateness, style, and plausibility of reports, proposals, or theories of other writers.
Writing	Communicates thoughts, ideas, information, and messages in writing; records information completely and accurately; composes and creates documents such as letters, directions, manuals, reports, proposals, graphs, flow charts; uses language, style, organization, and format appropriate to the subject matter, purpose, and audience. Includes supporting documentation and attends to level of detail; checks, edits, and revises for correct information, appropriate emphasis, form, grammar, spelling, and punctuation.
Arithmetic	Performs basic computations; uses basic numerical concepts such as whole numbers and percentages in practical situations; makes reasonable estimates of arithmetic results without a calculator; and uses tables, graphs, diagrams, and charts to obtain or convey quantiative information.
Listening	Receives, attends to, interprets, and responds to verbal messages and other cues such as body language in ways that are appropriate to the purpose; for example, to comprehend, to learn, to critically evaluate, to appreciate, or to support the speaker.
THINKING SKILLS	
Speaking	Organizes ideas and communicates oral messages appropriate to listeners and situations; participates in conversations, discussions, and group presentations; selects an appropriate medium for conveying a message; uses verbal language and other cues such as body language appropriate in style, tone, and level of complexity to the audience and the occasion; speaks clearly and communicates a message; understands and responds to listener feedback; asks questions when needed.

TABLE 6.1
(continued)

SCANS Foundation Skills	
Creative thinking	Uses imagination freely, combines ideas or information in new ways, makes connections between seemingly unrelated ideas, and reshapes goals in ways that reveal new possibilities.
Decision making	Specifies goals and constraints, generates alternatives, considers risks, and evaluates and chooses best alternative.
Problem solving	Recognizes that a problem exists (i.e., there is a discrepancy between what is and what should or could be); identifies possible reasons for the discrepancy, and devises and implements a plan of action to resolve it. Evaluates and monitors progress and revises plan as indicated by findings.
Seeing things in the mind's eye	Organizes and processes symbols, pictures, graphs, objects, or other information; for example, sees a building from a blueprint, a system's operation from schematics, the flow of work activities from narrative descriptions, or the taste of food from reading a recipe.
PERSONAL QUALITIES	
Responsibility	Exerts a high level of effort and perseverance toward goal attainment. Works hard to become excellent at doing tasks by setting high level of concentration, even when assigned an unpleasant task. Displays high standards of attendance, punctuality, enthusiasm, vitality, and optimism in approaching and completing tasks.
Social	Demonstrates understanding, friendliness, adaptability, empathy, and politeness in new and ongoing group settings. Asserts self in familiar and unfamiliar social situation; relates well to others; responds appropriately as the situation requires; takes an interest in what others say and do.
Self-Management	Assesses own knowledge, skills, and abilities accurately; sets well-defined and realistic personal goals; monitors progress toward goal attainment and motivates self through goal achievement; exhibits self-control and responds to feedback unemotionally and nondefensively; is a "self-starter."

Source: *Skills and Tasks for JOBS: A SCANS Report for America 2000,* Secretary's Commission on Achieving Necessary Skills, 1992.

 How can you develop and improve both your job-specific and transferable skills?

Skills Development.   In the case of job-specific skills, the best way to improve them is to actually use these skills on the job. This can be done through part-time work while in school, internships, cooperative education programs, etc., which we will discuss in more detail in the following section on experience. With transferable skills, you may need specialized educational assistance to develop your capabilities. For example, if you determine that you have a weakness in one of the foundation skill areas, such as reading or writing, it may be appropriate for you to take classes to help you improve these skills. Or it may be necessary for you to take a class on problem solving, or maybe managerial strategy. Possibly a management training program would help you, or attending a seminar on interpersonal skills development. Even reading one of the dozens of self-improvement books available could assist you in becoming more skilled in your weak areas. Various methods of skill enhancement exist; choose those that best suit you and make your quest for improvement an ongoing process.

Experience

The last of the functional qualities that we will discuss, and one which goes a long way toward determining your degree of marketability, is your previous work experience. Career planning experts agree that one of the best ways to increase your level of employability is to obtain work experience in your chosen occupation. Related work background allows you to develop your job-specific and transferable skills, while increasing your knowledge base. By actually working in the field you will be able to gain insight into the "real world." The information you obtain from your class work does not always give an accurate picture of what goes on in a given job. By acquiring firsthand experience, you are better prepared to "hit the ground running" when you accept your first full-time career position.

Employers look for this experience when hiring and will almost always give preference to someone who has it. With work experience on your resume, potential employers can see that you have worked in the field, were successful, and enjoyed it. Whether via a paid full-time or part-time job, or an unpaid position such as an internship or volunteer work, developing this functional quality can go a long way toward increasing your employability and guiding you toward successful employment.

As a college student, it is not always possible to find work that is directly related to your career choice. But even having worked in a field other than your chosen profession can prove very beneficial when searching for that first job after graduation. Most any type of work will help you to develop and utilize transferable skills that can be used in other occupations. Qualities such as leadership, teamwork, and problem solving can be developed through many different types of jobs. Work ethic and dedication can be demonstrated by employment in jobs typically associated with college students, such as cashiering or retail work. Some organizations actually prefer to hire an applicant who has worked in what some consider a "menial job," such as a fast-food cook or pizza delivery, while in college. They see these applicants as possessing drive and determination because they were willing to do whatever work was necessary to help them achieve their goal of graduating from college. When you are planning how to develop your employability, keep in mind that experience, as a functional quality, can mean more than just a job in the same occupational field.

Another outcome of gaining practical experience is that you are developing your network of references—people who can recommend you to a potential employer as someone who is knowledgeable, skilled, dedicated, hardworking, etc. You should never forget that one job can act as a stepping stone to another, and how effectively you perform your job determines the type of reference that you will get from your supervisor. Always, the individual who has good references from previous employers will be given preference over someone who has poor references or no references at all. Keeping this in mind can help you to see that there is value in any job you do, no matter how menial you think it is, and that it can play a part in determining how employable you are in the eyes of a potential employer.

WHERE TO BEGIN THE PROCESS OF DEVELOPING EMPLOYABILITY

In order for workers to compete in the high performance workplace of today, they need to possess certain qualifications that will enable them to work effectively within the context of this new work environment. As we have previously noted, these qualifications are significantly different from the ones that employers looked for just a few years ago. It is important to gain an understanding of what qualities are needed to become a high-performance worker in your chosen profession, and then to raise your employability rating by acquiring those attributes. So where do you begin the process of evaluation and planning to improve your employability rating? Once again the importance of self-assessment in career planning becomes apparent.

It is best to begin by addressing the generic components of employability—those qualities that will be needed in almost all jobs—and then look at how to acquire the skills and background specific to your career field. Below is an abridged version of the functional qualities we have thus far discussed and which have been identified as the critical elements needed for success in any job (Ramsey, 1994):

- Ability to work with all kinds of people
- Willingness to give 101%
- Enthusiasm and commitment
- Broad interests and experiences
- Capacity to change and learn new skills
- Excitement for learning and growth
- Problem-solving skills
- Ability to communicate effectively
- Capacity to be a self-starter
- Ability to work with minimum direction
- Dedication to quality customer service

In creating a plan for developing your employability, begin with these characteristics. Honestly and objectively assess how you rate in each of these areas. What are your strengths? What areas do you particularly need to develop?

After you have looked at these generic workplace requirements, shift your focus to your career field and find out what qualities are desired by employers in that field. Paying particular attention to your weaknesses, begin to devise a plan for acquiring and strengthening your skills in these areas. Review the functional qualities presented in this chapter to see what other areas you believe will need to be improved upon to increase your marketability. Exercise 6.1, Employability Checklist (at the end of this chapter), will help you to organize this information and create a plan for developing your employability.

SUMMARY

There are two major goals in the developing employability and job readiness stage. The first objective, and the focus of this chapter, is to create a plan to develop yourself into a marketable commodity by acquiring the assets that employers in your chosen field look for when hiring their employees. The second major goal of this stage is to prepare yourself for the job search process by learning how to write an effective resume and related employment letters, as well as developing your interviewing skills. This second component is covered in chapters 7 and 8.

Improving your level of employability includes assessing your functional qualities, which are the elements that employers look at when making hiring decisions. Functional qualities are the knowledge, skills, and experience that you bring to the workplace. Knowledge refers to the level of understanding you possess about your career field. Skills represent your ability to apply the knowledge you have acquired to a specific job. Skills, as a functional quality, are very broad in scope, and this chapter focuses extensively on this area because there are so many components to it. Experience, as the name implies, refers to the on-the-job training an applicant possesses. Employers look for this as a way of measuring how an applicant has performed in the workplace. Reference checking provides them with information they can use in making hiring decisions.

In order to make yourself more employable, it is imperative that you gain a strong understanding of what qualities you will need to become successfully employed in your field, and work toward acquiring those qualities.

EXERCISES AND DISCUSSION QUESTIONS

1. Imagine that you are a personnel manager, responsible for locating and hiring new employees for your organization. What skills or characteristics would you look for most in job applicants? Why do you feel that these qualities are the most important?

2. What functional qualities do you possess that you believe are the most marketable? How can these qualities help you in your chosen field of work?

3. Many of the competencies and skills identified in the SCANS report (Table 6.1) are needed by people as they engage in a program of career planning. Looking at the career development model (chapter 1), identify which of the SCANS skills you feel would be used in each stage. This will help you identify how these skills are used in everyday life.

4. After studying Table 6.1, pick out those areas that you feel are your weakest and describe how you could strengthen your skills in those areas.

Exercise 6.1   Employability Checklist

Having read chapter 6, you now have a better idea of the qualities employers look for when hiring their personnel. Make a list of all the things that you can do that would increase your "employability rating" and make yourself more marketable when you begin your job search. You may need to review the information presented in the chapter to refresh your understanding of functional qualities and the role they play in your level of employability. Follow the example below and develop a plan for acquiring the skills that will help you to become successfully employed.

Skill/Characteristic To Be Developed	How Can This Be Developed?

General Employability Elements *(those found in nearly all jobs)*

(Example) Acquiring information	*Take a class in how to use the Internet*

Job Specific Elements *(those particular to your career field)*

(Example) Gain accounting experience	*Obtain an internship during junior year*

Be certain to review and update your employability checklist on a regular basis. As you learn more about what knowledge, skills, and abilities are needed in order to become successfully employed, you can add them to your list.

Resume Writing

After completing this chapter you should understand

- *The format of the two most commonly used resume styles*
- *How to develop a resume that effectively portrays your skills and abilities*
- *The five characteristics of a well-developed resume*
- *How and when to use an electronic resume*

INTRODUCTION

 Can you present your qualifications effectively in writing?

We will now turn our attention to a very important aspect of the developing employability and job readiness stage: how to design a resume that presents your qualifications most effectively. A resume is a synopsis of you—your abilities, interests, education, experience, achievements, and goals. In addition to its use for employment application, a resume can be used when applying to graduate schools, entrance to scholastic organizations, or merely to keep a permanent record of your professional background and accomplishments. In this chapter we will focus on how to write a resume that will sell your qualifications to a prospective employer, thereby increasing the likelihood of being invited for an interview.

Selling is a key idea to remember when writing a resume. Just as a good advertisement presents a product in a very appealing way, so too should a resume. You should attempt to make yourself as attractive as possible on paper so that the employer feels as though she would be missing out by not interviewing you. Many people fall short in trying to do this with their resume. The best way to make yourself attractive on paper is to find out what the needs of the organization are and match aspects of your background, education, experience, accomplishments, etc., to these needs. By doing so, you improve your chances of moving past the screening stage to the interview stage, which is exactly what you want to accomplish.

Ideally you would have a separate resume for every job that you apply for, each designed to show how well your qualifications match up to the specific requirements of the position. However, it is not always feasible, because of the costs and time constraints involved, to develop a new resume each time you apply for a job. If you can do so, all the better, but with some time and thought, you can create a resume that will be acceptable for most job applications.

 What makes a resume a good resume?

CHARACTERISTICS OF A WELL-DEVELOPED RESUME

Merely putting information about your background on paper does not assure a quality resume. When putting together your resume, there are some important ideas to keep in mind. The following are five characteristics of a well-developed resume that you should incorporate into yours (Figure 7.1).

Concise/Scannable

If at all possible, you should keep your resume to one page in length. The reason for this is very simple: if it is too long, it probably will not be read. A good resume should be designed so it can be easily scanned. Studies show that personnel managers, and other hiring authorities, typically only give a cursory overview to a resume the first time they look at it. They are looking for key words and phrases indicating that this individual has the basic qualifications for the job. If the reader sees something that is appealing in the resume, only then will she go back and read it in more detail. Your job, then, in putting together a top-notch resume, is to make sure that the assets you possess that are most needed by the employer are apparent to the reader.

Talents, skills, experience, and other background that you possess that are desired by the employer should be highlighted in some fashion so as to draw attention to them. One good way to emphasize important material is to make use of **bold type,** *italics,* underlining, and other word processing techniques that cause the information to stand out. When someone is scanning a resume, there is a natural tendency for the eye to stop at anything that is different. The bold type in the following accomplishment statement is eye-catching and stands out considerably more than the same statement without the bold type.

Responsible for a **25% increase** in budgetary appropriations.

It is a good idea to use these types of techniques when developing your resume. Be careful not to use too many or the effect will be diminished. Properly done, this technique can change your resume from a good one to a great one.

Results Oriented

To the greatest extent possible, you need to present yourself as being a results-oriented person. This means that you should include in your resume significant accomplishments, goals you have achieved, and important tasks and activities that you have designed, implemented, directed, or coordinated. Employers look for individuals who can get things done, who take an active role in setting goals and completing tasks. You should include accomplishments and leadership roles from your previous work experience and extracurricular activities, committee assignments, etc., in building these concepts into your resume.

FIGURE 7.1
Characteristics of a
Well-Developed Resume

Characteristics of a Well-Developed Resume

Concise/Scannable

Results Oriented

Highlights Strengths

Shows Involvement

Aesthetically Pleasing

Don't sell yourself short here. What you may think was an unimportant assignment or a minor leadership position may be eye-catching to a recruiter. Take a good look at your educational background, work experience, and extracurricular activities, and include on your resume those things that present you as someone who gets things done.

Highlights Strengths

What have you done that is exceptional? Is there any aspect of your background that is particularly strong and would make you stand out from those with whom you would be competing for a job? Almost certainly there are some areas in which you are more accomplished or proficient than most people. It could be your grade point average or other scholastic achievement, work experience, or your record of leadership. If you have done an adequate job of self-assessment, you will be able to identify your strength areas and be able to convey them on paper.

Some people are afraid that by highlighting their individual strengths and accomplishments, they will come across as arrogant or boastful. One of the few places that it is acceptable for you to brag on yourself is on a resume. In all likelihood, what you are afraid will appear as bragging will be looked upon by others as an impressive accomplishment. So whatever your strengths, aptitudes, or special talents, be sure that they are made known to the reader of your resume.

Shows Involvement

When recruiting recent college graduates, some employers feel the most important part of an applicant's resume is the section on extracurricular activities. These employers look to see whether or not a prospect was active in organizations outside of the classroom. Having done so demonstrates a willingness on the part of the individual to work with others as part of a team to achieve common goals—characteristics that will be needed in order to become a productive member of the employer's organizational system.

Therefore, when writing your resume, be sure to include any involvement in student organizations, campus politics, religious organizations, community service programs, etc. This could very well make the difference between being accepted or rejected for an interview.

Aesthetically Pleasing

Your resume is a reflection of yourself. When you create your resume, you are putting yourself on paper, and it is from this document that prospective employers will often form their first impressions of you. When you mail a copy of your resume in application for a job, you are introducing yourself for the first time, and as the saying goes, "You only have one chance to make a good first impression." So don't blow it by submitting an inferior or shabby-looking document.

Your resume needs to be attractive and well organized (Figure 7.2). This means that there should be adequate margins, with information centered and balanced on the page, high-quality paper should be used, and the type itself should look appealing and smudge-free. Avoid using dot matrix printers because they do not typically produce the neat, clean look of a laser-printed document. Making ample use of "white space," that part of the paper that contains no printed material, also makes for a clean look and has the effect of causing the information to stand out and become more "scannable." Submitting a resume that is poorly printed or that uses an inconsistent format can cause a negative impression in the mind of the reader—an impression you definitely want to avoid.

Making typographical errors and using poor grammar on your resume are other sure ways to find yourself excluded from consideration for jobs. Even if you are qualified for a job, a resume full of errors can prevent you from even having the opportunity to interview for it. One personnel director takes an especially dim view of those who mail resumes to

FIGURE 7.2
How to Design an
Eye-Catching Resume

To ensure that your resume is appealing and eye-catching use these guidelines and design tips.

- *Incorporate "white space" into your resume design.*

- *Design your resume for easy scanning.*

- *Emphasize major data by underlining, capitalizing, or using italic or bold type.*

- *Center and balance your resume on the page.*

- *Use 8 1/2" x 11" bond paper in a conservative color (white, gray, or ivory).*

- *Use a laser printer or professional printing service.*

- *In describing job duties avoid pronouns such as I, we, they, etc., which are understood. Begin job duties with action verbs.*

- *Keep your resume to one page if at all possible. Long resumes may not be read.*

- *Have others proofread your resume to be sure there are no errors on it.*

her firm without checking to make sure that all errors have been removed. When she receives a resume or cover letter in the mail that contains typographical errors, she underscores the errors in red pen, mails it back to the applicant, and does not invite the person for an interview. Her rationale is that if the person is going to produce an error-filled document before being hired, he would also do so after being hired. The moral of this story is clear: Make certain that there are *no* errors on your resume or any other correspondence you use in the job search process. Proofread your resume again and again before submitting it, and have at least one other person do the same. Many times people overlook a mistake because, having seen it written incorrectly often enough, their mind does not interpret it as an error. Therefore you should always have someone else, and preferably more than one person, proofread your work.

If you do not have access to the necessary word-processing software and laser printing equipment, seriously consider having your resume professionally typed and printed. The money you invest will be well worth it. The career planning and placement office at your school can usually provide this service for a nominal charge or can refer you to others who can help. If you do not have access to this type of service on your campus, there are numerous printing companies that offer resume services. Do not try to get by with a second-rate resume produced on a poor-quality dot matrix printer at home. Most of the applicants with whom you will be competing will have a professionally typed resume, and you don't want yours to be substandard.

RESUME FORMATS

There are various formats you can use when writing your resume. Each has advantages, and all have at least one inherent disadvantage—they cannot take the place of a face-to-face meeting with a prospective employer. It is hard to sell yourself if you can't talk directly with the person you are trying to sell to, and for this reason many people do not like resumes. It is very difficult to convey interpersonal skills, enthusiasm, and professional image on paper. It is extremely rare that a resume alone will get you a job. What a good resume can do is get you an interview, which will then allow you to convey the qualities just listed.

We will focus on two resume formats—reverse chronological and functional—because these represent the most universally accepted styles. We will also look at how to develop an electronic resume which is used for computerized job searching. Today employers are increasingly making use of applicant tracking systems, which allow them to use computers to search for qualified applicants faster and more efficiently than ever before.

Reverse Chronological Format

The reverse chronological resume is the most widely used format, and for recent college graduates or those who are beginning their professional career, it typically represents the best method for presenting strengths and accomplishments. As suggested in the title, the reverse chronological resume is designed to present background information in reverse order of time. The information is provided with the most recent experience and education appearing at the top of each section, with earlier experience and education listed in the reverse order of occurrence. In this format, functional qualities—knowledge, skills, and experience—are presented by dividing them into sections that show where and how they were acquired. As a general rule, reverse chronological resumes will contain three to seven sections, depending on individual background and accomplishments. Outlined below are the major sections of this resume format and the information that should be presented in each. Examples of reverse chronological resumes are shown on pages 85–87.

Sections in the Reverse Chronological Format

Identifying Information.   This part of the resume contains your name and contact information. If you are in school and live away from home, include both your school and permanent addresses. Always include your telephone number with area code. If this information changes, correct it on your resume as soon as possible. It is important that you remain accessible to any employer who is interested in talking with you. It often happens that an employer wants to interview an applicant but cannot get in touch with her, either because the contact information is outdated or the individual is away from home for a period of time. Employers will rarely try more than two or three times to contact an applicant for an interview. If they get no response they will move on and have another applicant fill the interview spot. When writing your resume, you may want to put the phone number of a relative or friend who can locate you when you are away from home. In doing so, list this number below your home phone number with the word "Message" written beside it.

Objective.   If you go to any book store and look through the books on resume writing, you will see this section called by many different names, including professional objective, career interest, career goal, and interest area. For the sake of simplicity, we will refer to this section simply as the *objective*. The purpose of the objective is to let the reader know the type of job you want. It should convey career direction and, at the same time, present you as goal oriented.

It is preferable to have a separate resume with an objective linked specifically to each job you apply for. This tells the reader the type of job you want and makes your goals appear compatible with what the organization has to offer. If you are applying for a job with a bank, for instance, your objective should illustrate your interest in the job and/or the banking industry. For example: To obtain a position in entry-level management in the banking industry.

The problem with putting a specific objective on your resume is that you cannot use that same resume in applying for just any position. For example, if your resume contained the objective listed above, you could only use it for banking jobs and would need to have a separate resume printed with a different objective on it for nonbanking jobs. This can become expensive if you apply for a number of jobs in different industries.

You may therefore elect to not include an objective on your resume, since this has the advantage of allowing you to use one resume when applying for different types of jobs without incurring the expense of having your resume retyped and printed. This is acceptable and, financially, may prove to be your most practical option. If you choose to omit the objective from your resume, you should make sure that the type of position you want is clearly spelled out in your cover letter. You do not want the reader to guess as to the type of job you are looking for.

You may want to consider having two or three resumes with differing objectives that are general enough to be submitted for several different types of jobs. Each resume could be designed to emphasize varying aspects of your background so that those aspects most appropriate for a certain type of job would be accentuated. This has the benefit of providing you with resumes appropriate for a number of different types of positions, but without the need for innumerable and costly revisions each time you apply.

When writing an objective, your goal is to succinctly describe the type of position you would like to obtain. If your goal is to find a position as a sales representative, your objective could be, quite simply: To obtain a position as a sales representative. If you specifically want to work in pharmaceutical sales, your objective could be something like: To obtain work as a pharmaceutical sales representative. The degree of specificity you place in your objective is up to you. If you are only interested in working for a major company, you could use something like: To obtain a position as a sales representative for a leading consumer products firm.

If you have a geographical preference for where you want to work, you may want to put that in your objective too. However, be aware that the more specific your objective is, the fewer the number of jobs for which you will be considered.

One mistake that you should avoid is to list a very broad, all-encompassing objective statement that tells little about the type of job you desire. For example, the following objective doesn't say anything of importance: To obtain a challenging position where I can use my talents for the betterment of the organization. This could describe any job and does not give the reader any notion of the type of position desired. It is better to leave it off altogether than to write an objective that is vast and all-encompassing.

Education.   This section provides information on the individual's level of educational attainment. For college graduates, the information should include the name of the educational institution(s) attended; the degree attained, if any; the major field of study; and the date of graduation. It is also appropriate in this section to list any significant academic achievement awards that have been received, such as graduating summa cum laude or with similar honors. This information should be placed under the degree title. Do not document all of your awards and achievements under this heading. List only those academic honors of special merit here; save the rest for the subsequent section entitled Honors/Awards.

If there are specific courses you have taken that a prospective employer needs to be aware of, it is appropriate to list them under the Education heading in a subsection called Relevant Courses. This section is optional and should only be included if you have taken classes that are in addition to what would normally be expected in a given curriculum. If you have a degree in accounting, then it is pretty well understood that you have had basic accounting courses. Include only classes that are relevant to the type of job that you are applying for and which the reader would not normally be expected to know about.

You may also want to include information concerning your high school education. Follow a similar format to the one above; however, it is not necessary to be as descriptive. The name of the high school, location, and date of graduation will generally suffice. Again, significant honors should be included.

Another category that can be placed in this section is Special Skills. These are abilities that have been acquired through education, but which are not apparent as a consequence of your degree. Examples of these are computer skills, knowledge of specific software programs, foreign language proficiency, or any other distinctive skills or knowledge. These skills may be very important to an employer and could also give you an advantage over the competition when interviewing.

Work Experience.   This section is a summarization of the jobs you have held. Particular attention should be paid to the writing of this section because it is one's work experience that many organizations look at when deciding which applicants to interview. As was discussed earlier in the developing employability and job readiness stage, gaining practical experience in your occupational field is one of the best ways to improve your chances of getting a job offer. As a general rule, employers prefer an individual who has prior related work experience. This person will usually bring experience and insight that can be directly translated into productive time for the company. Less time spent on training means a quicker return on investment for the employer.

What this suggests in resume development is the need for determining which aspects of your work experience are most closely related to what the employer wants, and emphasizing these aspects. Since every employer is not looking for the same qualifications, the rationale for writing a separate resume for each job is apparent—the more you can tailor your resume to the needs of the employer, the higher the probability of obtaining an interview. A well-written cover letter can help you tie in your background with the needs of the employer. Chapter 8 discusses how this can be done most effectively.

The information presented in the Work Experience section should begin with the name of the organization and your title. If it is not obvious, you should include the name of the city in which you were employed. The people who read your resume may be unfamiliar with the company or organization for which you worked, or if you worked for a large, national company that has offices in many different cities, they may not know in which city you were employed. Further, if the organization for which you worked is small or has little name recognition, you may want to include a brief description of the organization. For example: JTM Corporation (Financial consultants).

For each job listed you should provide the dates of employment. Some people advocate that if you have had a series of short-term jobs, or if there are gaps in your employment, it is best to leave off the dates of employment. However, most employers want to know the amount of job experience an applicant has, and you should extend them the courtesy of providing this information. For those who are traditional-age college students, gaps and short-term jobs will rarely be an issue anyway, because it is understood by employers that college students generally have not had any long-term jobs. Internships usually don't last more than a semester and part-time jobs are seldom long term. Even for those who are several years into their career and have had an opportunity to establish a work background, it is generally not advisable to try and disguise or "doctor" their resume to cover employment gaps or a sporadic work background. The potential negative consequences outweigh the possible benefits of providing misleading information.

There is an exception to the rule of providing dates of employment for each job listed. If, after listing your key jobs, you have some less important positions you want to include, it is acceptable to group these under one heading without dates. In this case you could do something like this: Part-time employment while in school includes cashier, lifeguard, waitress, stock clerk, and babysitter.

With the exception of the above example, where jobs are grouped in order to prevent an overly long resume, you should always include the duties of each job you held. Do not assume that the reader will know what the duties of the position were by the title. Duties and responsibilities can vary widely within job titles. An account executive with one firm does not necessarily have the same duties as someone with the same title at another firm. Choose the most important aspects of each job, making sure to include those which a potential employer would deem meaningful, and include these under the Duties section.

FIGURE 7.3
Action Verbs

accomplished	critiqued	implemented	projected
achieved	created	improved	promoted
acquired	decided	increased	proposed
administered	defined	initiated	purchased
advised	delivered	inspected	rated
aided	demonstrated	installed	recommended
affected	designed	instituted	related
analyzed	determined	instructed	recruited
applied	developed	interpreted	regulated
appraised	devised	interviewed	reported
arranged	diagnosed	introduced	researched
assessed	directed	invented	resolved
assigned	disapproved	investigated	reorganized
assisted	discharged	joined	reviewed
assumed	distributed	led	revised
assured	dramatized	maintained	saved
attained	drafted	managed	scheduled
awarded	edited	mapped	secured
bought	enlarged	modernized	selected
budgeted	enlisted	monitored	served
brought	ensured	motivated	sold
chaired	established	named	solved
changed	estimated	negotiated	sorted
classified	evaluated	obtained	sought
closed	examined	observed	specified
communicated	expanded	operated	spoke
compared	expedited	ordered	straightened
coached	explained	organized	strengthened
completed	facilitated	originated	structured
conceived	financed	participated	suggested
concluded	forecasted	perceived	summarized
conducted	formulated	perfected	supervised
continued	founded	performed	targeted
contracted	gathered	persuaded	taught
controlled	governed	planned	tested
converted	graded	prepared	trained
convinced	guided	presented	updated
coordinated	handled	presided	utilized
corrected	harmonized	processed	verified
counseled	headed	produced	wrote

When writing this section of your resume, you are encouraged to make use of action verbs (Figure 7.3). Words like *accomplished, achieved, designed, implemented, directed,* and *managed* have the effect of painting an image of you in the mind of the reader as a dynamic, results-oriented individual. It adds vitality and enthusiasm to what may otherwise appear as dull. Which of the two examples of the same job duty is more appealing?

> Accounts payable
> or
> Managed a seven person Accounts Payable department

Another example:

> Telemarketing
> or
> Increased telemarketing sales by 45%

Yet another:

> Inventory control
> or
> Designed and implemented an inventory control program resulting in a
> 15% decrease in lost and misdirected shipments

In each case, the second example makes use of action verbs which result in a more powerful statement and, in the last two examples, combines the duty with an accomplishment, making for an even more enticing statement.

Types of Work Experience. Work experience can include a variety of different types of jobs. Full-time and part-time jobs, temporary summer jobs, internships, and cooperative education positions all fall into the category of work experience. Even volunteer work qualifies for this category. Just because you didn't get paid for doing a certain job does not mean that it is unimportant and should be excluded from your resume. If you have any work experience that you did not get paid for, you may want to identify it as a volunteer position, but do not omit this type of work from your resume, especially if it was a community service job. Some employers want to hire civic-minded people who are willing to donate their time to a worthy cause. Just as in a paid position, a supervisor for a volunteer position can attest to your work habits and might turn out to be a pivotal reference for you when you begin interviewing for professional jobs.

This idea of including "low-level" jobs on your resume also applies to the jobs you may have had while working your way through school. Many students are embarrassed that they were "just a busboy" or "only a waitress," and feel this type of job should be left off of their resume. However, keep in mind that working in what you think was a "menial" job could demonstrate to a prospective employer that you are dedicated enough to work your way through school and could be seen as a positive reflection of your work habits.

Optional Sections.

The sections that we have thus far discussed are essential components of any reverse chronological resume. With the exception of the objective, each section needs to be included on this type of resume. We will now turn our attention to some optional sections that you may or may not include on your resume, based on your individual background and accomplishments.

Honors/Awards. If you have received any academic, extracurricular, or civic honors, you should list these under this heading. Include awards such as scholarships, honor society memberships, scholastic achievement awards, civic awards, etc. These awards will help to demonstrate your abilities and accomplishments to a prospective employer. It looks very impressive to have a resume that is loaded with these types of accomplishments.

Recognition and awards of this sort are especially beneficial for those who are just beginning their career. Why? As a new graduate, the Education and Work Experience sections of your resume are going to look quite similar to that of many other recent graduates. In other words, most will have a college degree and some type of job experience. You can set yourself apart from the crowd by having an impressive list of achievements, honors, and awards.

Activities. As we discussed earlier in this chapter, one of the things that some employers look for in prospective employees is involvement. It is important that you include this type of background on your resume. Teamwork and an ability to work well with others are critical skills necessary for success in the workplace. Actively participating in extracurricular activities demonstrates that the individual has these skills. This is seen as an asset in the eyes of most employers. Examples of the types of extracurricular activities you should list in this section include membership in campus organizations, civic and service clubs, social fraternities or sororities, and professional affiliations. Leadership roles, such as president, vice president, etc., are especially impressive and should also be included in this section.

There are other sections that you can include on your resume if you feel it is appropriate. An Accomplishments section could be included if you have a number of achievements that do not fit under any of the other sections. Some people will want to include a section on Hobbies and Interests.

Some professionals in the field of career guidance believe that this sort of information is unnecessary and advise that you leave it off of your resume, while others maintain that it is helpful in order for the potential employer to gain a better understanding of who you are. The choice is yours. If you do not have any additional information that is appropriate, or if you are uncomfortable about revealing this type of information, then you need not include it. If you are not opposed to it and it does not overburden your resume, then put it in. A strong argument can be made for either case, so use your best judgment about adding additional categories. If you feel there is justification for including additional categories, then do so.

References.   Here again we run into an area of disagreement among the "experts." Some advocate that references should not be listed on the resume, but rather should be included on a separate sheet of paper. Others argue that, if space permits, it is perfectly acceptable for references to appear on the same page with the rest of the resume information. Again, you will need to decide what works best for you. If you have a very short resume that takes up considerably less than one page, you may want to place your references on the same page, if for no other reason than to balance out an otherwise scanty document. If your resume already fits neatly on the page, or if you just want a separate References page, then, by all means, you should do so. Neither is inherently wrong, so use your common sense and personal preference when deciding.

While there are no strict rules regarding where to place your list of references, there are some guidelines regarding whom to list. Your best sources for references, and the ones that carry the most credibility, are people who have been in a supervisory or evaluative position over you. These *professional references* include former bosses, supervisors, teachers, and other administrators who know you. These are the people who can offer an evaluation of your work ethic, dedication, punctuality, ability to get along with coworkers, etc. In the eyes of employers, these individuals constitute the best, most credible references.

Another category of references are those people with whom you are associated other than as a pupil, employee, supervisee, etc. These *personal* or *character references* are those neighbors, friends of the family, or similar acquaintances, who can comment on your integrity, attitude, and other personal characteristics. This does not include family members. Never list a member of your family as a reference; even the most inept worker will get a good recommendation from his mother. Hiring authorities will have no confidence in such a reference. Include only nonfamily members who know you and can make a positive statement about your character.

There are two final items to keep in mind when listing references. First, always ask before including anyone as a reference, since they may not want to provide a recommendation for you. It could be disastrous for you if that person is called by a prospective employer and he refuses to give you a reference or worse, gives a very unflattering evaluation. Second, it is a good idea to submit a resume to each person whom you ask to be a reference. This is especially true if it has been some time since you worked for or were associated with these people. They are entitled to know more about you and what you have been doing recently. It also gives them a more comprehensive picture of the person they are recommending.

Figures 7.4–7.6 present sample reverse chronological resumes.

Functional Resume Format

The second type of resume format that we will look at is known as the functional resume. The focus of this kind of resume is to identify the skills that you possess (i.e., managerial, sales, planning and organizing, computer programming, etc.) and develop the resume

JIM SMITH
123 Riverwood Drive
Anytown, USA 12345
(xxx) 555-7756

EDUCATION	**Bachelor of Science**, May 1995
	University of Nebraska, Lincoln, Nebraska
	Major: Geology Minor: History
	GPA: 3.75/4.00
	Computer Skills: Lotus 1-2-3, COBOL, SPSS
EXPERIENCE	**Intern**, May 1994–August 1994
	Carson Geological Consultants, Denver, Colorado
	- Assisted Senior Geologist with collection of field samples
	- Performed laboratory chemical composition tests
	- Input data for statistical software package
	- Met with clients to discuss project status
	Student Assistant, September 1992–May 1994
	University of Nebraska, Department of Geology
	- Compiled and indexed statistical information from soil sample tests
	- Inspected and cataloged incoming soil samples
	- Streamlined procedures for testing and grading core samples
	- Wrote reports summarizing results of soil sample tests
	Head Lifeguard, Summer 1991 and 1992
	Riverwood Swimming Pool, Denver, Colorado
	- Responsible for safety of swimmers
	- Taught beginning and intermediate swimming classes
	- Supervised four lifeguards
HONORS/ ACTIVITIES	President, Geology Club
	Kappa Delta Psi, Geology Honorary
	Student Ambassadors
	History Club
	Tutwiler Scholarship Award
	Dean's List (six semesters)
	Photography Club

References available upon request

FIGURE 7.4
Sample Resume 1: Reverse Chronological Format

Edward Poole
389 Cordelia Lane
Elm City, USA 23456
(xxx) 555-8942

Objective: Seeking a position in the field of personnel management.

EDUCATION

<u>**Mississippi State University**</u>, Starkville, Mississippi
Bachelor of Science, Personnel Management, May 1995

Relevant coursework includes:
- -Personnel Administration
- -Organizational Behavior
- -Benefits Administration
- -Labor-Management Relations
- -FORTRAN
- -Managerial Strategies

EXPERIENCE

Stock Clerk, Parker Hardware, Columbus, Mississippi, August 1994–May 1995
- Received and cross-checked incoming merchandise with purchase order
- Stocked showroom shelves
- Redesigned warehouse storage space to more efficiently accommodate incoming and outgoing merchandise
- Cleaned showroom daily

Intern, Foster Manufacturing, Inc., Jackson Mississippi, May 1994–August 1994
- Assisted Personnel Manager with daily operations
- Electronically processed time cards for payroll
- Entered employee benefits information into computer database
- Interacted with insurance company personnel on workman's compensation claims

Cashier, Bob's One-Stop, Starkville, Mississippi, September 1992–May 1994
- Served customers
- Operated cash register
- Stocked shelves
- Purchased inventory
- General janitorial duties

CAMPUS ACTIVITIES

- Vice-president, Student Business Association
- Student Government Association representative
- Crises Line volunteer
- Homecoming Committee

FIGURE 7.5
Sample Resume 2: Reverse Chronological Format

Carolyn Turner
1818 21st Street
Ocean City, USA 12345
(xxx) 123-4567

Objective

To obtain a position in health care administration.

Education

Bachelor of Science, Health Care Management
Boston College - May 1995
3.94 GPA

Central High School
Ocean City, USA
Graduated May 1991

Work Experience

January 1994– Present	**Wal-Mart**, Boston, Massachussetts *Sales Associate* Assist customers with purchases, stock shelves, operate cash register, maintain appearance of showroom.
Summer 1993	**Jolly Time Daycare**, Ocean City, USA *Daycare Worker* Responsible for welfare of five to eight children, developed recreational activities, supervised play. Also handled secretarial/clerical duties, such as answering phones, maintaining records, etc.
Summer 1992	**Sanderson Motor Company**, Ocean City, USA *Receptionist* Answered phones, routed calls, kept records of salespersons daily work schedules, filed sales and title information.

Extracurricular   Chess Club
                             Debate Team

Activities   Intramural sports
                             Student Recruitment Team

FIGURE 7.6
Sample Resume 3: Reverse Chronological Format

Functional Skills List

Here are a few examples of skills that may be used in developing a functional resume:

Accounting	Information	Research
Administration	Management	Sales/Marketing
Analysis	Interviewing	Supervision
Budgeting/Finance	Leadership	Teaching
Communication	Management	Testing/Assessment
Counseling	Personnel Management	Training/Development
Creativity/Innovation	Planning/Organization	Troubleshooting
Crisis Management	Problem Solving	Writing/Editing
Human Relations	Public Relations	

FIGURE 7.7
Functional Skills List

around those skill areas (Figure 7.7). When using the functional format, you pick out those skills which you possess and would like to portray to an employer and then cite examples from your background that show how you have demonstrated those skills.

When comparing the functional with the reverse chronological resume format, the latter presents information primarily from the perspective of *where* one has acquired qualifications (education, work experience, etc.), while the functional resume focuses more on the particular *skills* the person possesses that would benefit the employer. In order to make effective use of the functional resume, you should have background and experience to draw from in order to portray your skills. Someone who has few or no examples to cite from his background that can illustrate his skills should not use the functional format.

Sections in the Functional Resume Format

Identifying Information and Objective.   Developing the Identifying Information and Objective sections is done exactly the same as outlined under the reverse chronological format. Use the information from the reverse chronological format presented in this chapter when writing these two sections of the functional resume.

Functional Skills.   As previously noted, the functional format uses a person's skills as the primary means of presenting qualifications for employment. This section lists the individual's skill areas followed by experiences which serve to illustrate those skills. It is important when using this format that each skill area be supported by a brief description of how the worker has demonstrated that skill. A claim of "research skills" has no merit unless the reader can see how the writer has demonstrated research ability. When using this format, the writer should be sure to include examples, with each skill highlighted, of how she has performed that skill. Example:

> Leadership
> -Served as president of the German Club
> -Coordinated Homecoming Day activities
> -Organized blood drives for the Red Cross
> -Elected chairman of the student advisory council

Work Experience.   The work experience section of a functional resume is typically less detailed than that of a reverse chronological resume. Generally only the name of the organization, title, and dates of employment are provided. Some may choose to provide more information, but usually those who choose this format have done so in order to focus attention on their skills rather than on their work history. Therefore this section of the functional resume is relatively brief. Some even leave this section off completely, choosing to accentuate the skills section. This is not recommended however. An employer evaluating the resume of a prospective employee is interested in knowing where he has worked and this information should be provided.

Optional Sections.   In addition to the sections outlined above, the functional resume may also include one or more of the optional sections discussed under the reverse chronological format. For information on these, please refer back to that portion of this chapter.

A word of warning when using the functional format: Be careful about being overly wordy. It is quite easy to become long-winded when trying to effectively showcase your skills. Some people get carried away when using this format and end up writing a lengthy narrative of their background. As often as not, this kind of resume gets filed away without being read. Remember the rule regarding the average length of time that a resume is initially scanned? You have just a few seconds to sell yourself on paper, so you need to make your resume readable while highlighting your assets. Few people will take the time to read a long paragraph-form resume. If you choose this format, keep it brief.

In this chapter we have not addressed the functional resume format to the same extent as we did with the chronological format, and the reason is simple—this textbook is designed primarily for college students and recent graduates and, for most of you, the chronological resume is the recommended style. It allows you to succinctly outline your background and training for a particular job, while accentuating those attributes you possess that would be beneficial to a prospective employer. A functional resume is better suited for an individual who has a significant amount of experience, whereby specific work-related skills that have been developed can be highlighted, and examples included of how these skills have been demonstrated on the job. While some college students, especially returning adult students, may have significant work experience where they have had the opportunity to demonstrate their skills, most do not, and a well-developed functional resume will be hard to produce.

You be the judge of which format is better for you. Decide which format does a better job of selling you, and go with it. Regardless of the format you choose, remember that in developing an effective resume, you should find out what qualifications are desired in a particular job and fit your background to those requirements. The more you appear to match the duties and qualifications of a job, the better your chances of obtaining an interview.

Figure 7.8 presents a sample functional resume.

Electronic Resume

Technology in the workplace is continually being applied in extraordinary ways that make work easier and more efficient. The field of recruitment and hiring is no exception. Today employers are increasingly making use of computers to read resumes and screen applicants for job openings. Applicant tracking and resume scanning software programs utilize the incredible speed computers offer in searching resume databases to locate individuals who meet given criteria. Instead of spending valuable time reading and sorting through stacks of resumes, personnel managers and other hiring authorities can quickly access large numbers of resumes and almost instantly retrieve those that most closely match their job requirements.

  How does an electronic resume differ from a traditional paper resume?

The electronic resume is not necessarily a different format from the ones we have discussed, but rather it uses a different style of writing. A good electronic resume can use either the reverse chronological or functional resume format; the difference is in how it is

Margaret Carter
101 Pine Circle
Omaha, Nebraska 12345
(xxx) 555-1234

PROFESSIONAL
OBJECTIVE   A position in human resources management.

SKILLS   *Training and Development*
-Designed and implemented a career development program
 used companywide to assist employees with setting and
 obtaining career goals.
-Administered and taught computer literacy classes for staff
 development program.
-Developed training manuals for new employees.
-Responsible for budgeting funds for various training programs.

Personnel Management
-Recruited, interviewed, and screened job applicants.
-Administered preemployment tests.
-Directed payroll disbursements.
-Coordinated third-party benefits administration.
-Approved and scheduled employee vacations.

Public Relations
-Chairperson for countywide adopt-a-school program.
-Cochairperson for county American Heart Association.
-Served on Chamber of Commerce industrial
 development committee.
-Acted as company spokesperson for community affairs issues.
-Wrote press releases.

WORK
EXPERIENCE   *Assistant Personnel Manager*, June 1993–Present
Avery Products, Sioux City, Iowa

Personnel Specialist, August 1990–May 1993
Avery Products, Sioux City, Iowa

Records Clerk, September 1987–May 1990
Spartus Corporation, Lincoln, Nebraska

EDUCATION   *Bachelor of Science, Human Resources Management*
University of Nebraska, May 1990

References available upon request

FIGURE 7.8
Sample Resume 4: Functional Resume Format

presented. Joyce Lain Kennedy and Thomas J. Morrow have written a book entitled *The Electronic Resume Revolution* (1994) which describes how to best write this kind of resume. In their book the authors identify a key difference between a standard paper resume and an electronic resume. Where paper resumes encourage the use of action verbs when describing one's background (i.e., *directed, improved, increased*), an effective electronic resume makes use of *keywords.* Keywords are typically nouns that describe or "label" people as to the type of jobs they have held or the kinds of duties they have performed. The reason for including these on an electronic resume is that the applicant tracking software uses keywords that have been selected by the personnel administrator to search a database of resumes to find the candidates who most closely match the qualifications for a job.

For example, if the personnel director of a retail department store chain wants to hire someone for a retail manager trainee position, she could enter keywords such as *retail, sales,* and/or *management* into a computer using applicant tracking software. She might even want to specify a particular type of degree such as *B.S. in Business Management* to further refine the search. The computer will quickly search the database and provide a list of those applicants who have these keywords on their resumes. The benefits of this type of system are obvious—considerably less time is spent manually searching through stacks of resumes trying to find the best applicants. The computer can search more resumes in less time, increasing the productivity and efficiency in personnel departments.

Here are other examples of how keywords can be used with applicant tracking software to help employers search for qualified people in various fields:

Occupation	Keywords
Banking	Financial management, credit management, loan officer, estate planning, trust services
Sales	Outside sales, inside sales, B.S. marketing, promotional strategies
Personnel management	Human resources management, employment regulations, EEO, staffing, benefits administration

These examples offer guidelines for the types of terms that are used as keywords. The thing for you to remember when writing your individual electronic resume is to include a variety of descriptive terms that depict your work experience and skills. The more of these words that are included on a resume, the greater the likelihood of a match between them and the keywords specified in the search. Kennedy and Morrow (1994) even advocate the use of industry jargon in writing an electronic resume—something that has generally been considered taboo on paper resumes. Employers may include jargon as keywords in their electronic search and therefore it is suggested that jargon be used in writing electronic resumes.

Due to the high cost of applicant tracking and resume scanning software, relatively few employers presently use this technology. But as with most technological advances, costs will come down and, as they do, more and more organizations will automate this aspect of their operations. In Kennedy and Morrow's (1994) book, it is suggested that job hunters use both the traditional paper resume and an electronic version. You should use your judgment when deciding when to use which version. If you know for certain that your resume will be scanned and placed in a computer database to be used with an applicant tracking system, then naturally you should use the electronic version. If you are applying for employment and you are taking your resume directly to an individual, then you may want to use the traditional format. A third option, and one that can be used when you do not know whether your resume will be manually or electronically processed, is to take a creative approach and design one that incorporates guidelines from both styles. Using a combination of keywords (as recommended for the electronic resume) and action verbs (as recommended for the traditional version) an excellent resume can be designed that contains the best qualities of both resume styles.

SUMMARY

Knowing how to write a high-quality resume that effectively presents your qualifications is one of the best ways to increase your chances of being selected for a job interview. Conversely, a poorly written resume is one of the best ways to ensure that you will not be considered. This chapter identified five general characteristics of a well-developed resume: concise, results oriented, highlights strengths, demonstrates involvement, and aesthetically pleasing.

Two major formats for writing a resume were presented in this chapter: the reverse chronological and the functional. Each takes a different approach to presenting one's qualifications. In addition, the concept of an electronic resume was introduced. This kind of resume is designed to be used in conjunction with the latest computer technology that allows resumes to be placed in a database and retrieved by employers as they "electronically" search and recruit new employees.

EXERCISES AND DISCUSSION QUESTIONS

1. Write a resume that would be appropriate to submit in applying for professional-level jobs. If necessary, use the information from Exercise 3.2, Personal Information Form, to assist you in recalling all of the pertinent information that should be included.
2. Compare and contrast the reverse chronological resume format with the functional format. What are the advantages of each? Which format do you believe is best for you at this stage in your career? Why?
3. "Resumes don't tell the whole story," complained one personnel manager. What are some possible explanations for what he could have meant by this?
4. If you were applying for a job today, and the application procedures ask for three references, who would you list? What do you think they would say about you?
5. If you were a personnel manager in an organization, responsible for screening job applicants, what would you look for when reviewing resumes? Why are these things important? In what way is a person's resume indicative of the type of worker he would be?

Employment Correspondence

After completing this chapter you should understand

- *How to write an attention-grabbing cover letter*
- *The difference between a cover letter and a letter of inquiry*
- *How to write a thank you letter following an interview*

INTRODUCTION

 Can you effectively convey your qualifications in a business letter format?

Career planning experts know that effective letter writing is directly linked to a successful job search. Learning how to write first-rate employment letters can help you to more effectively sell yourself to potential employers. A poorly written letter, on the other hand, can be all that is needed to eliminate you from consideration for a job. In this chapter we detail the most common types of employment correspondence—cover letter, letter of inquiry, and thank you letter—and illustrate how best to write each one.

COVER LETTER

We begin our discussion of employment correspondence with the *cover letter.* This type of communication, also known as a *letter of application,* is used in conjunction with a resume when applying for a job. Anytime a resume is submitted in response to a job announcement it should be accompanied by a cover letter. This document is designed to introduce your resume, and thereby yourself, to the hiring authority and show why you are a good candidate for the position.

The cover letter should follow standard business letter format. Three topics should be addressed. First, you need to tell the reader why you are writing and you should include the title of the position you are applying for. It is also important to include where, or from whom, you learned of the job. If you read about the position in a newspaper advertisement or similar listing, include the name and date of the publication. If you saw the job announcement in your college or university placement office, indicate so in this first section. If you were referred by someone who knows the person to whom you are writing, be certain to include the name of this mutual acquaintance. A great number of jobs are obtained by this kind of "third-party" referral. The employer reading the letter is much

more likely to stop and pay attention to your letter if she recognizes the name of someone she knows, especially if it is someone whose opinion she respects.

It is acceptable to indicate in this part of the letter *why* you are interested in this particular job. If it offers you the opportunity to work in a field that you have been preparing for through college, let the reader know. If it is the company or organization itself that interests you, then you may want to indicate this. A simple statement such as,

> My education and experience in electrical engineering has given me a solid foundation in this field of work

may be enough to whet the reader's appetite and keep her reading. Try to come up with a statement in this first paragraph that will catch the reader's attention and entice her to look further at your qualifications.

The second point that needs to be included in a cover letter may, in fact, be the most important. After telling the reader why you are writing, you must show how you can contribute to the organization by giving strong evidence of your ability to do the job. In writing this portion of the cover letter, it is important that you know what the most essential requirements of the job are and relate aspects of your background to these requirements. Doing so will help you to convince the reader that you are an excellent candidate for the position.

Be certain to emphasize your achievements in this section. Showing how you have demonstrated your talents and skills by citing specific accomplishments from your background is a good way to grab the reader's attention. Awards of special merit, exceptional academic achievement, and superior performance on the job are all examples of accomplishments that can make you stand out from the crowd. Use these types of selling points from your background to jazz up your cover letters.

While these things can be advantageous, you should take caution to avoid overselling. Do not get too bogged down by itemizing every detail of your qualifications. Choose two or three major selling points that you possess and, in one or two sentences each, demonstrate their appropriateness for the job. Your resume should give most of the information the reader will need, so keep your letter to one page or less and avoid needless duplication of information. A long, detailed cover letter is similar to no cover letter—both are hard to read!

While an excessively long cover letter can be counterproductive, you can also make the mistake of going to the other extreme by not selling yourself strongly enough. A one paragraph, "here is my resume call me if you are interested" cover letter is ineffectual. Put time and thought into writing this portion of the cover letter and use the methodology outlined above; it can be just the thing needed to catch the eye of the hiring authority and get your foot in the door.

The last item of the cover letter is the close, and it is here that you should ask the hiring authority for an interview—tactfully. How should this be done? A technique used by some in the sales profession offers insight into why "asking for the interview" is important and how it should be handled. Many sales training programs teach that to "ask for the order" is a tried and true technique for making a sale. Take, for instance, a salesperson who works for a tool manufacturing company who is trying to convince the purchasing agent of a hardware store to take on a new line of hand saws. After introducing and describing the product, he invites the buyer to try it. He might say something like, "Mike, let me send you four dozen of our tempered steel Super Saws and let you see how well they sell."

What, you may ask, does this have to do writing a cover letter? Well, actually quite a lot, because the same selling principle applies in both situations. Both you and the hardware salesperson are increasing the probability of a positive response by merely asking for what you want. The salesperson knows that he will make more sales by asking the buyer for an order than he will by merely informing him of the product and hoping that he buys. So it is with the personnel manager or hiring authority to whom you send a cover letter. Because of your request, she may be prompted to schedule you for an interview. Now, realistically, sometimes it may take more than merely asking in the cover letter; you may need to follow up with a phone call. But if one phone call results in an interview with a top-notch company, it would certainly be worth it. Let us now look at how to best "ask for the interview."

In closing your cover letter, you should finish on a confident note that leaves an impression in the reader's mind that you would be worthy of an interview. If you have done an effective job in the body of the letter, the reader will already want to talk with you. However, as with the salesperson, you should end with a specific request and not ruin an otherwise strong letter with a weak ending. "Thank you for your consideration" does not request an interview, nor does it generally convey the kind of message that you want to present to the reader. In the final paragraph you should request a face-to-face interview in a positive tone that implies that such a meeting would be mutually beneficial.

> I am confident that I have the background and ability to be successful in
> this position. I would like to further discuss with you how I could be an

asset to XYZ Corporation. I will contact you on or before June 15 to schedule an appointment. In the meantime, if you have any questions, or would like additional information, please do not hesitate to call.

When you use this type of close, be certain to follow up and contact the person by the date specified. Lack of follow-through can portray you in a very negative light.

For some this type of close seems too forward. They are not comfortable with such a direct approach. If you are of this opinion, you may want to try a different, less direct approach. After making a convincing argument for your qualifications for the job, you could conclude with something such as

I would appreciate the opportunity to speak with you face-to-face concerning how I could be of benefit to XYZ Corporation. I have enclosed my resume which will offer additional information on my qualifications for the job of Project Supervisor. I look forward to hearing from you soon.

While not quite as assertive as the previous example, you have still asked for an interview and, if you so decide, you can still contact the hiring authority by phone later to follow up on the status of your application. As with the resume, double-check your cover letter for any errors. Even a single mistake looks bad and could keep you from being invited for an interview.

The sample cover letters in Figures 8.1, 8.2, and 8.3 offer examples of how to write a persuasive letter. Use these as guidelines and put your own individual touches on each one so that you present yourself in the most appealing way possible.

REQUIREMENTS/CREDENTIALS COMPARISON

A tool that can be quite effective and which may be used in conjunction with the cover letter is the *requirements/credentials comparison*, which, as the name implies, illustrates how an individual's qualifications for a job match up with the requirements of the position. The information is presented in a concise, easy-to-read, comparative format, and may be included as an addendum to the resume and cover letter. This technique is best suited for those occasions when your background and experiences closely parallel the requirements specified in the job description.

In designing this document, make a list of each of the requirements of the job for which you are applying and type these on the left side of a page. Directly opposite each requirement, on the right side of the page, briefly describe the qualifications you have that meet each requirement. Table 8.1 is an example of a requirements/credentials comparision.

This comparative profile gives the hiring authority a quick overview of your qualifications as compared to the organization's needs. Again, this technique should not be used for every job application. An entry-level position that specifies few requirements is not a good place to use this technique. If the only requirement put forth in the job description is a baccalaureate degree, then you will not have enough on the "requirements" side to create a "credentials" side. Also, if you are only marginally qualified for the position, this approach will not work well because the matches between the two sides of the page will be weak. It is best to use this only when there are several qualifications listed for which you possess appropriate background, experience, or skills.

123 Riverwood Drive
Anytown, USA 12345
January 17, 19xx

Ms. Charlotte Green
Employment Director
Environmental Consultants, Inc.
P.O. Box 7692
Denver, CO 12345

Dear Ms. Green:

Please consider my qualifications for the position of *Environmental Assessment Coordinator* in your Southeastern Region. Nancy Spearman of your Atlanta office told me of the position and recommended that I contact you for additional information.

I will graduate this May from Jonesboro College with a bachelor's degree in geology. My experience as an intern with Carson Geological Consultants, as well as in the Jonesboro College Department of Geology, has provided me with a strong foundation in the field of environmental impact research. My specialty area of soil composition analysis should prove beneficial in performing the duties of the Coordinator. The enclosed resume provides additional information on my background.

I am interested in learning more about the position and would like to talk with you about my qualifications. I will contact you next week to further discuss the possibility of employment with Environmental Consultants. If you have any questions, please feel free to call me at the number on my resume.

Sincerely,

Jim Smith

FIGURE 8.1
Sample Cover Letter 1

389 Cordelia Lane
Elm City, MS 12345
April 7, 19xx

Mr. Joseph Hornsby
Yellow River Manufacturing
P.O. Drawer 179
New Orleans, LA 12345

Dear Mr. Hornsby:

I am applying for the position of Human Resources Specialist advertised in the April 6 edition of the *Daily Tribune*. I am a graduate of Mississippi State University with a degree in Personnel Management. I believe that my background and education make me a strong candidate for this position.

During my internship with Foster Manufacturing in Jackson, Mississippi, I gained considerable insight into the operations of a personnel department. I learned how to electronically process time card information, and I also became familiar with filing workman's compensation insurance claims. During my tenure, I revamped the claims filing system, speeding up processing time. I have enclosed my resume which provides more information on my qualifications.

I would appreciate the opportunity to speak with you further concerning my qualifications for the position. I will contact you the week of April 14 to schedule an interview. In the meantime, please feel free to call me if you have any questions at (601) 555-8942. Thank you for your consideration.

Sincerely,

Edward Poole

FIGURE 8.2
Sample Cover Letter 2

4001 45th Street, N.
Bakersfield, FL 01234
June 1, 19xx

Winston Byrd, Vice President
TJM Group
P.O. Box 18127
San Francisco, CA 12345

Dear Mr. Byrd:

I am writing in response to your advertisement for an Account Executive in the September 2, 19xx issue of *The Chronicle*. I am originally from San Francisco and it is my goal to return to the area.

My educational background and work experience have helped me to acquire the skills necessary to perform the duties of this position. My degree in Advertising and Public Relations has given me a strong understanding of the PR field. Additionally, my involvement in campus organizations, combined with significant public speaking experience, has enabled me to develop strong leadership and communication skills. This background would help me to join a firm such as TJM Group and quickly contribute to the organization.

I will be in San Francisco the week of September 10, and would like to meet with you to discuss the position and my qualifications. I will contact you prior to my arrival to schedule an appointment. In the meantime, feel free to contact me at the number on my resume if you have any questions.

Sincerely,

Tim McKinney

FIGURE 8.3
Sample Cover Letter 3

TABLE 8.1
A Sample Requirements/Credentials Comparison

Jane Smith's Qualifications for Employment as a Contractor Sales Representative with Turner Building Products, Inc.	
Job Requirements	*My Qualifications*
Four-year degree	B.S. Marketing
Two years sales experience	Three years experience in sales of building materials
Knowledge of building codes	One year experience as Assistant Building Inspector
	Completed six-week building code training program
Computerized purchasing experience	Completely familiar with JobTrax purchasing software

LETTER OF INQUIRY

A second type of correspondence we will discuss which is very similar to the cover letter, yet it used for a slightly different purpose, is the *letter of inquiry*.

 How does the letter of inquiry differ from the cover letter?

The cover letter format just discussed is used when applying for a particular job opening for which an organization is actively recruiting and trying to fill through advertising, word of mouth, or other means. The letter of inquiry, on the other hand, is used when you want to make contact with a company/organization in which it is unknown to you whether or not there is an opening. For example, if you are interested in working for Acme, Inc., as an accountant, but you are unaware of any specific job openings, you should write a letter of inquiry to the company in which you outline your qualifications for an accounting position. As with the cover letter, you begin the body of the letter by explaining your reason for writing. In this case, you inform them of your desire to work for Acme as an accountant. You may want to indicate why you have selected Acme as a recipient of your letter of inquiry. It could be their reputation in the industry, or perhaps your interest in their particular field of work.

You should next provide a brief explanation of your qualifications for employment in such a position. Unfortunately you will not have the luxury of fitting your background to a job description as you would in the case of a cover letter. However, you should highlight your unique knowledge, skills, and experiences in such a way as to appeal to the hiring authority if she were attempting to fill an accounting position. Follow the guidelines suggested with the cover letter to portray yourself as a strong candidate for employment. Emphasize your achievements, specific accomplishments, and/or superior job performance as examples of why you are worthy of consideration.

As with the cover letter, you need to conclude the letter of inquiry with a strong finish and, again, request an interview. Even if the company is not currently in the market for an accountant, they may be in the near future, and if so, you will be in an advantageous position if you have already had an interview and made a positive impression. Figure 8.4 shows a sample letter of inquiry.

783 Dogwood Circle
Santa Fe, NM 12345
October 1, 19xx

Ms. Evelyn Burkett
Distribution Manager
Computronix Corporation
1400 Industrial Boulevard
Phoenix, AZ 12345

Dear Ms. Burkett:

I am writing to inquire about job opportunities with Computronix. I am a recent graduate of Arizona State University with a bachelor's degree in Business Administration. I learned of Computronix through an article in *Southwest Business Journal*. This article cited your firm as an industry leader in the field of distribution and transportation.

I am very interested in working in the distribution management field. My senior project was to develop a resource distribution computer program. With the help of my project supervisor, Dr. Blackburn, this program was adopted by two local manufacturing firms. Both have reported increased efficiency in their distribution departments.

I would appreciate the opportunity to talk with you about employment possibilities within your organization. I will contact you the week of October 13 to schedule an appointment. Please feel free to call me in the meantime if you know of any immediate openings. Thank you for your consideration.

Sincerely,

James Cole

FIGURE 8.4
Sample Letter of Inquiry

THANK YOU LETTER

The last type of employment correspondence we will discuss is the *thank you letter*. The thank you letter is a short note that is written after the job seeker has interviewed for a position. Its primary purpose is to extend gratitude to an individual, or group of individuals, who have taken the time to meet with you to discuss employment possibilities. This simple letter is one of the most overlooked aspects of the job search process. Relatively few people take the time to write a thank you letter following an interview. Ironically, it is this short note that oftentimes makes the difference between receiving a job offer and being rejected. Recruiters, personnel managers, department heads, and other hiring authorities are just like everyone else—we all want to be appreciated. When you go out of your way to let an interviewer know that you appreciate his time, that person tends to take notice.

 How should a thank you letter be written and when should it be sent?

We discuss employment interviewing in the next chapter, but for now let us assume that you, the job seeker, have just finished an interview with a company representative. Before you leave the interview, make sure that you have the interviewer's name, title, and company mailing address. Many times the interviewer will give you her business card, providing you with all necessary information, but if not, ask for it. If you are interviewing through your college or university's placement office, the placement personnel should have the necessary information. If you are interviewing at the employer's place of business, you can ask the secretary/receptionist for this information. How you get it is not as important as just making sure you get it. Within a couple of days following the interview, you should write a thank you letter to each of the people to whom you spoke. Use the following guidelines to write your letters (see Figure 8.5).

After the appropriate date, inside address, and salutation, you should begin your letter with a brief acknowledgment and reminder of when and for which job you applied.

> I would like to express my thanks to you for taking the time to interview me last Tuesday for the position of Computer Systems Programmer.

You may follow with a statement of what benefit you gained from the meeting.

> The information and assistance you provided were extremely helpful.

Any other statement or specific reference to something that happened in the interview that you feel is applicable can also be inserted here.

As previously noted, the primary purpose in this letter is to extend gratitude. A secondary, yet important element is the opportunity to express continued interest in the position and possibly include a short statement about your qualifications for the job.

> I remain very interested in the opportunity with Computer Data Systems.
> I feel confident that my background and training would make for an excellent match with the duties of the position.

Limit your sales pitch to one or two points and then close the letter with a final paragraph of confident expectation.

> I look forward to hearing from you concerning my future with CDS, Inc.
> Again, many thanks!

389 Cordelia Lane
Elm City, MS 12345
April 17, 19xx

Mr. Joseph Hornsby
Yellow River Manufacturing
P.O. Drawer 179
New Orleans, LA 12345

Dear Mr. Hornsby:

Thank you for taking the time to meet with me on Thursday. I enjoyed having the opportunity to learn more about Yellow River Manufacturing. The tour of the plant facilities was very interesting and enlightening.

With a greater understanding of your organization and the duties of the Human Resources Specialist, I am certain that I could more than adequately perform the responsibilities of the position. As we discussed during the interview, my training and work experience have included many of the same duties of the Specialist.

As per your request, I have asked the Records Office to forward a copy of my transcript to you. You should be receiving it within the next few days. If you need anything else, please call. Thank you again for your time and interest.

Sincerely,

Edward Poole

FIGURE 8.5
Sample Thank You Letter

Some people prefer to write, rather than type, their thank you letters. This is one of the few employment-related letters in which it is acceptable to do so. If you prefer a more personal touch, then don't hesitate to handwrite your thank you letters.

There are several other types of employment correspondence: follow-up letters, acceptance letters, letters for declining a job offer, letters to delay the organization while you consider an offer, etc. We have omitted these types of correspondence because they are not used to the same extent as the others. If, however, you find yourself in need of more information on how to write these types of letters, there are numerous books available that will be of assistance. Check with your local bookstore or library, both will have resources to guide you in this area.

SUMMARY

Knowing how to effectively correspond with potential employers can play a major role in determining how successful your job search will be. The cover letter and letter of inquiry are both a form of correspondence that is used to introduce an individual to a potential employer. The cover letter is designed to be used by job seekers when applying for a position that is currently being advertised or otherwise recruited for by an employer. The letter of inquiry is for use by job seekers who are just making contact with an organization to inquire about the possibility of employment with that firm. In this case, the individual typically is unaware of any specific job openings, but is "putting out feelers" just in case there are any unannounced openings.

The thank you letter is also presented in this chapter. Its purpose is primarily to extend gratitude to the person, or persons, with whom you have met to discuss employment possibilities. The letter also offers the applicant the opportunity to briefly express his continued interest in and qualifications for the job.

EXERCISES AND DISCUSSION QUESTIONS

1. Find a job vacancy or internship announcement for a position in which you would be interested in applying. Using the guidelines provided in this chapter, write a cover letter in application for this position. The purpose is to gain practice in writing a letter that effectively sells you to a potential employer.
2. Address this question: If an applicant for a job submits a strong resume, is a cover letter even necessary? Why or why not?
3. How does a letter of inquiry differ from a cover letter? When should each be used?
4. Assume that as a consequence of your cover letter in question 1, you were invited for an interview with the organization. You feel as though the meeting went extremely well and you are interested in pursuing the position further. Using the guidelines provided in this chapter, write a thank you letter to the interviewer.
5. Some people prefer the typed, business format when writing a thank you letter, while others prefer a handwritten one. Which one do you prefer? Why?

9

Interviewing

After completing this chapter you should understand

- *How to best prepare for an employment interview*
- *The typical interview formats*
- *Techniques for handling yourself during an interview*
- *What factors should go into job offer consideration*

INTRODUCTION

 Can you relate your story line effectively to employers?

The job interview. This event draws a variety of emotional responses from those about to participate in one. Some will feel excited about the possibility of being selected to interview for a rewarding job. For others, the reality of being evaluated to determine whether or not they "measure up" causes anxiety, doubt, and distress. For these people the face-to-face interview creates fear and apprehension because they feel unprepared to talk with someone that they don't know, from an organization that they are unfamiliar with, concerning a job that they probably know little about. Also adding to their stress is the understanding that the interviewer may ask them difficult questions that they may not be able to adequately answer, and that their performance is going to be compared to other applicants who may be more qualified and better prepared. Those people who picture the interview in this way are setting themselves up for an anxiety-producing encounter.

The good news is that it does not have to be this way. The key to overcoming the fear associated with the interview process is to acquire information and prepare accordingly. Those people who have gone to the trouble to gather information pertinent to the interview, and to prepare for it, are the ones who feel most confident and are the ones who are most successful.

THE INTERVIEW

Interviewing is a two-way exchange of information. The applicant is learning about the position and the organization, and the interviewer is learning about the applicant. This meeting gives the applicant the opportunity to relate his story line to a potential employer. A *story line* is a summarization of the assets you have to offer to an organization, specifically your functional qualities—knowledge, skills, and experience.

Employment interviewing is the central component of the job search process. Much of what a job seeker has accomplished by following the career development model guidelines—preparing a resume, identifying prospective companies/organizations, pursuing job leads, mailing letters, and making phone calls—has been done in order to gain an interview. While all of the preparation in the world cannot guarantee someone a job offer, there are several techniques that can be used that will help increase the likelihood of receiving an offer of employment. Let's look at how you can develop your interviewing skills so that you have a better chance of landing the job of your dreams. In doing so, we will break down the interview process into two parts: the preparation stage, and the actual face-to-face interview.

INTERVIEW PREPARATION

Arguably the most important part of the interview process is the preparation. Prior to the actual interview, a job seeker should take steps that will increase his level of confidence and allow him to become more proficient at interviewing. Presented here is a two-step process that is designed to do just that. We call these simply *confidence building steps* and they are

1. Do your homework
2. Practice interviewing

Confidence Building Step 1: Do Your Homework

The first step refers to the importance of learning as much as you can, prior to the actual interview, about the company, the position, and if possible, the person or persons with whom you will be meeting. A good understanding of the position and the organization will enhance your ability to link your functional qualities to the requirements of the job, thus enabling you to better sell yourself. Where can you locate this type of information? Let's begin with the position itself before turning our attention to sources of information on the organization and the interviewer.

Information on the Position.   By learning all you can about the position for which you are applying, you strengthen your ability to describe to the interviewer how your background and skills fit the job. It is difficult to answer the question "What qualifies you for this position?" if you do not know what the position entails. If the job is advertised, the announcement will usually give basic information on the duties and responsibilities of the job. But, if possible, you may want to talk to someone who works in a similar position to find out specific job duties that may not be listed in the announcement. If the job is listed with your college or university's placement office, there will be a copy of the job description on file. These descriptions are a good place to start, but they are not necessarily the most comprehensive source of information. Talk to some of the placement personnel in the office; they may be able to offer some additional information that is not common knowledge. Be inquisitive. The more you learn, the better.

Information on the Organization.   How about information on the company? Corporate recruiters and other hiring authorities frequently ask applicants the question "What do you know about our company?" It is very impressive if you have done some research and can relate facts, figures, and other company information to the interviewer. In all likelihood you will not tell them anything that they do not already know, but you will have demonstrated that you are interested and motivated enough to do some research and have a basic knowledge of the company/organization. Never make the mistake of being unable to tell an interviewer something about her organization. Most of the people with whom you will be competing for this job will have done this type of research, and you do not want to be the only uninformed applicant.

 What should you learn about a company/organization prior to meeting with a representative for an interview?

In addressing the question above, obviously the more information you have, the better prepared you will be for any questions that might be asked of you about the employer. While you can't learn everything about the organization, Figure 9.1 specifies some of the pertinent information you may want to learn. You need not be concerned with being able to recite all of this information to a prospective employer (some of it you will learn during the interview); however, it is important for you to have a fundamental knowledge of the organization and be able to relate this to the interviewer if asked. Some interviewers are not only impressed by those who take the initiative to find this sort of information, they expect it. It would be unpleasant, at best, to find yourself in an interview with someone like this and be forced to admit that you know nothing of the firm. Even if you are not asked, it would be wise to let the interviewer know that you have done some research into her organization. Making a comment to a recruiter such as, "I read in the latest issue of *Business Week* that Johnson Industries is planning an expansion into the overseas market," accomplishes two things. First, it lets the interviewer know that you have taken the time to do some research into the company and, second, it provides a topic

FIGURE 9.1
Pertinent Information for
Interview Preparation

> Products and/or services
> Industry ranking
> Number of employees
> Location of corporate/regional headquarters
> Competitors
> Training programs
> Current news items
> Future plans
> Number of plants/stores/offices, etc.
> History of organization (founder, growth, etc.)
> Name(s) of top corporate officers
> Subsidiaries/parent companies

of conversation during the interview in which you can learn more about the firm. This sort of advanced preparation can make a very favorable impression and weigh heavily in the employer's hiring decision.

 Where can I find specific sources of information on employers?

There are numerous sources of information on employers. This is especially true for larger organizations, but even smaller regional and local companies offer literature and other information on their products, services, organizational structure, etc. Again, start with your college/university career planning and placement professionals. These individuals can lead you to the information sources that are available on your campus. If you decide to strike out on your own fact-finding mission, here are some good sources of information, many of which are available in the business or reference section of the library.

Annual Reports. Almost every large and many medium-size companies produce an annual report that details financial information, past-year activities, future plans, etc. These can give a good picture of the company and provide a topic of conversation when the interview takes place. If your library does not have an annual report for a specific company, call the company and request one. Many companies will provide one at no charge.

Directories. These books provide a wealth of information on a great many of the employers in this country. *Standard & Poor's* has a series of directories that furnish corporate information on most of the major companies operating in the United States. You can obtain information such as the company's history, products and services, sales figures, number of employees, locations of offices and facilities, etc. Also provided is biographical information on the company's executive officers.

The *Moody's Manuals* are another excellent source of company information. These manuals offer information on corporations traded on the U.S. stock exchanges and are divided into occupational categories such as banking and finance, transportation, and industrial firms. Here you will find company histories, subsidiary operations, principle plants, products and services, and names of officers.

The *Thomas Register, Dun and Bradstreet, Ward's Directory,* and numerous others can be helpful in "doing your homework" on prospective employers. Ask the librarian or career resource personnel on your campus for assistance.

Periodicals. Yet another printed source of company information are the myriad newspapers, magazines, journals, etc., that contain articles about your prospective employer. One of the best ways to locate articles on specific companies is to make use of the computer-ized periodical databases located in many libraries. In using these computers, you simply type in the name of the company or organization that you want information on and the computer provides a listing of articles that have been written about that company. This re-source allows you to brush up on current topics and prepare for a discussion of issues facing the organization.

People. People can also provide helpful information on an employer. By talking to someone who has worked for or is familiar with an organization, it is possible to learn im-portant facts that could prove beneficial. If you know of someone who can give you this kind of information, ask them for help. These people can often provide "inside informa-tion" that is unavailable from other resources. This technique is especially appropriate in finding out information on smaller, local firms on which there is little or no data, statis-tics, or other information available in print. As the majority of companies in this country are classified as small businesses, this will quite often be the case. If you find that the li-brary has no information on a firm, ask around to see if you can locate someone who cur-rently works for or has previously worked for the company. While maybe not the most objective source of information, current and former employees could prove to be a quite helpful resource.

If this proves fruitless, try yet another approach: call the company and ask the secre-tary or receptionist for some assistance. Most organizations have company information literature, as well as product/services brochures that they use as sales and promotional material. If so, either go by and pick up these materials or ask the secretary to mail them to you. The information you acquire will be better than no information at all.

Understand that, in some instances, you may not be able to find any helpful informa-tion on the organization with which you will be interviewing. If this is the case, the next best thing is to find out what you can about the industry so that you will be somewhat knowledgeable of the general area of business, and then you can use the interview to find out more about the company.

Confidence Building Step 2: Practice Interviewing

The second confidence building step in interview preparation is to practice interviewing. This represents one of the most important, yet overlooked aspects of the interviewing process. Just as great orators practice and rehearse what they are going to say before giving a speech, you should likewise practice prior to interviewing for a job. The ability to interview is a skill and, as with any skill, the more you practice, the more proficient you will become, and your level of confidence in your ability to interview effectively will in-crease proportionally. This step represents one of the very best approaches you can take for improving your ability to sell yourself to prospective employers. And of course, the better the job you do of selling yourself, the more job offers you will receive (Figure 9.2).

 What are the most effective methods to practice interviewing?

Knowledge of Self + Knowledge of Organization + Preparation = Dynamite Interview!

FIGURE 9.2
Formula for Interview Success

In most interviews, the majority (though not all) of the communication takes place in the form of an interviewer asking questions and the applicant responding. Although this may seem a little one-sided, it is nonetheless, the format of most interviews. Therefore, a good portion of your preparation should focus on addressing these questions.

The first step to be taken in interviewing practice is to make a list of questions that a potential employer might ask you during an interview. You can start with the list of typical interview questions shown in Figure 9.3. But do not limit your list to these alone; think of specific questions that someone could ask you about your background. Put yourself in the shoes of the interviewer; if you were doing his job, what questions would you want to ask? Write these down on your list. Without too much effort you can come up with a list of 50 or more questions.

Next, prepare an answer for each of the questions on your list. These answers should be honest, well thought out, and should present your knowledge, skills, and experience in a positive manner. Make an outline of the points you want to make in answering each question. By doing this, you will have a very good answer already prepared and you will not have to fumble over your words during an interview trying to come up with an answer on the spur of the moment.

Making this list of questions actually will not be very difficult. In the majority of cases, the interviewer will cover the same basic information:

- You (your background)
- Us (the organization and job)
- What you can do for the organization

1. What are your greatest strengths?
2. What are your greatest weaknesses?
3. Why are you interested in this job?
4. Why did you choose your major?
5. Why did you choose this career?
6. What are your short-term goals?
7. What are your long-term goals?
8. What motivates you?
9. What two or three accomplishments have given you the most satisfaction?
10. Are you willing to travel?
11. Are you willing to relocate?
12. Describe a major problem you have encountered and how you dealt with it.
13. How has your college experience prepared you for this career?
14. How do you determine success?
15. What do you know about our organization?
16. What factors are most important to you in your job?
17. Why should I hire you over anyone else?
18. What have you done that shows initiative?
19. What did you like about your previous jobs?
20. What did you dislike about your previous jobs?
21. What classes were you most interested in? Why?
22. What would your former coworkers say about you?
23. How well do you work under pressure?
24. What are your salary requirements?
25. Tell me about yourself.

FIGURE 9.3
Typical Interview Questions

Knowing this, and following the guidelines described above, you should be able to anticipate and prepare for 80–90% of interview questions—maybe even 100%!

Keep in mind that developing answers to potential interview questions does not mean fabricating information. Some people believe that they can enhance the possibilities of getting a job offer by exaggerating their background and experience. This type of thinking can be very costly, especially if you are hired under false pretenses and your employer subsequently discovers your dishonesty. Come up with honest, informative answers that accurately portray your background and abilities.

Finally, you should practice your answers, refining them so that you are able to convey exactly the ideas you want. As we pointed out in our discussion of cover letters in chapter 8, it is sometimes advantageous for a job seeker to apply techniques used by those in the sales profession. Many successful salespeople utilize what is known as a "canned" sales presentation, meaning that the salesperson develops a sales pitch that highlights the important features and benefits of his products and services. He can then give his presentation to any number of prospective customers, making improvements and modifications where he sees fit to meet the needs of the client. Interestingly, the key to a canned sales presentation is that it does not sound canned, meaning that, with practice, the salesperson makes his presentation very polished and convincing.

A similar concept applies to interview preparation. After you have completed your list of potential questions and feel like you have come up with solid answers, you should spend time memorizing key points to each answer and then practice answering these questions as if you were actually in an interview. This enables you to give your "sales pitch" very effectively.

There are several techniques that you can use to polish your presentation skills. One method is *mock interviewing*. Many college placement offices offer this service where you can practice your interviewing skills by playing the role of an applicant for a fictitious job while a staff member acts as the interviewer. Afterwards, your performance is critiqued and suggestions for improvement are made. If this service is not available through your school, have a friend or family member play the interviewer's role and, if possible, make a videotape of the session so that you can go back and evaluate your performance. This allows you to check your posture, hand gestures, facial expressions, etc. Listen closely to your answers. Do they say what it is that you want to convey? Make notes of the things that you want to do differently when you are in an actual interview.

Another suggestion, if a video camera is unavailable, is to make an audio cassette recording of your practice sessions. While you will not be able to see yourself, you can hear your answers and, again, make changes that will improve your presentation. One final practice technique you can employ is to sit in front of a mirror and rehearse your answers. Although you will probably feel stupid at first watching yourself talk to a mirror, you have the luxury of getting immediate feedback on how you will look to an interviewer, and then, if necessary, you can make improvements in your interview style.

Once again, the benefit of these exercises is that when you are asked a question you will not have to be concerned with whether or not you are giving the best answer—or worse—giving a stupid answer! To the individual conducting the interview, you will come across as knowledgeable, articulate, and bright. And you will drastically reduce the number of times you find yourself after an interview thinking things like "I wish I had said. . . ."

Admittedly there are going to be times when questions will be asked of you for which you are unprepared, and there are even some interviewers who take pleasure in asking difficult and unexpected questions. When this happens, take a second or two and organize your thoughts; do not feel as though you have to immediately start answering the question. It is perfectly acceptable to pause for a moment or two and think about your response. You may want to say something like "That's a good question, I haven't thought about that before," then organize your thoughts for a few seconds and give the best answer you can. This "think before you speak" approach will help you give a better answer than merely blurting out the first thing that comes to mind, and may possibly prevent you from saying something that could eliminate you from consideration.

It can be argued that all of this preparation is too much trouble and overly time consuming. But look at it from this perspective: if you can dramatically improve your chances of getting the job of your dreams by merely spending a few hours of preparation time, wouldn't it be worth it? For most people, years of schooling have gone into just getting the opportunity to interview for a particular job, so why not invest a few more hours to sharpen your skills and gain an advantage? As with any skill, those who prepare for and practice interviewing will be more successful than those who do not.

Having completed the two confidence building steps, you will be significantly better prepared for the interview and, as such, your level of confidence will be higher. While confidence, in and of itself, will not guarantee you a job, an obvious lack of confidence can, most assuredly, hurt your chances. By using the principles outlined in the confidence building steps you will be better prepared to demonstrate your qualifications for a job and sell yourself to potential employers.

Questions for the Interviewer

In preparing for an interview, it is a good idea to make a list of questions you may want to ask the interviewer. These can include questions you have about the organization, the position, career paths, relocation, etc. (Figure 9.4) Nearly all interviewers will begin to wind up an interview by asking you if you have any questions. By asking questions, you not only acquire information, you are also demonstrating interest. Interviewers generally like this. So have a few questions prepared ahead of time, and if you have unanswered questions when the interview is over, use this opportunity to ask them.

During the first interview, avoid asking questions related to salary and benefits. You should already have a general idea of what the salary range is, and by asking you run the risk of appearing to have a what's-in-it-for-me attitude. For now, you want to demonstrate what you have to offer the employer, not dwell on what you can get out of the job. Oftentimes the interviewer will bring up the subject of compensation and benefits during the first interview; if so, it is then perfectly acceptable to discuss it. How to handle questions of salary is discussed later in this chapter.

1. What are the duties of the job?
2. What are the opportunities for advancement?
3. To whom would I report?
4. On what criteria would I be evaluated?
5. How much responsibility would I have as a new employee?
6. Why is this position open now?
7. How much travel is involved in this job?
8. How will the first weeks on the job be spent?
9. Is it your policy to promote from within?
10. What characteristics do you believe are needed to be successful in this position?
11. Does the organization support continued education?
12. What kind of training is provided?
13. What happened to the person previously employed in this position?
14. What are some of the problems people in this position encounter?

FIGURE 9.4
Questions to Ask the Interviewer

THE FACE-TO-FACE INTERVIEW

Most of our discussion in this chapter has been concerned with the preparation aspects of the interview process. Now we will turn our attention to the actual interview and begin by taking a look at the types of interview styles that one might encounter in a job search.

Interview Styles

The format of the interviews that you will experience in your job hunting will vary widely; usually this is a reflection of the individual, or individuals, conducting the interview. The format refers to the way in which the interview is conducted and is defined by the intent of those who perform the interview. In other words, the manner in which interviews are conducted is determined by what the interviewers want to find out from the applicants. The most common interview formats are the guided interview, the unstructured interview, and the stress interview.

The *guided interview* is the most commonly used format. In this approach, the interviewer has a set agenda of topics and questions that she wants to cover with the applicant. Typically this type of interview begins with the interviewer telling the applicant something about the organization and the position. She then begins asking questions about the applicant and his background in a effort to determine his qualifications for the job. In addition to qualifications, the interviewer is evaluating the applicant on things such as personal appearance, communication skills, personality characteristics, etc. She will usually conclude the interview by asking if the applicant has any questions.

The next format is the *unstructured interview*. As we pointed out earlier, most interviews follow the format of the interviewer asking a series of questions and the applicant responding to each. Sometimes, however, an interviewer will expect the interviewee to set the agenda and will do so by asking a very broad, open-ended question such as "Tell me about yourself?" By doing this, the interviewer, in effect, turns the interview over to the applicant by allowing her to choose the topics of discussion. This type of interview can be difficult to handle for the applicant because she does not know which aspects of her background the interviewer wants to hear about.

If you find yourself in this type of unstructured interview where you do not have specific questions to address, it may help to ask a question of the interviewer. "What aspect of my background would you like to discuss?" puts the responsibility back on the interviewer and gives you more insight into the type of information he wants. This makes it somewhat easier on you because you do not have to address such a broad question, hoping that you are giving the desired information.

Some interviewers will not be more specific and you may still have to answer this type of ambiguous question. One approach you may want to take is the "resume review," where you verbally outline the information on your resume, emphasizing the specific knowledge, skills, and experience you possess that you believe will be most needed in that particular job. Taking about three to five minutes, explain why you are an excellent candidate for the job. When you are finished, again put the ball back into the court of the interviewer by asking something like "Are there any areas you need me to elaborate on?" or "What else would you like to know?"

The last interview style we will discuss is the *stress interview*. The intent of the interviewer who employs this method is to introduce a degree of tension and anxiety into the interview in order to see how the applicant reacts to a stressful situation. This technique is often used for screening individuals for high-stress jobs. The procedure usually involves two or more interviewers who bombard the applicant with tough questions, or put him into a difficult hypothetical situation and ask him how he would handle it. Demanding a quick response, not allowing the applicant time to consider his answers, and even insults are characteristics of a stress interview. If you find yourself in one of these types of interviews, remember, the worst thing you can do is to lose your composure or to try to retaliate. It is not personal. You have not been singled out because they do not like you. You are merely being tested. Answer the questions to the best of your ability and stay calm and unruffled. As much as anything, they want to see how well you can keep your composure under stress.

Interview Day

The big day has finally arrived. All of your preparation has come down to this one day. There are two more things that you will need to think about before you leave for the interview: what to take with you, and what to wear. First, what to take.

Generally one or more of the following will be needed:

- Several copies of your resume (There may be more than one interviewer.)
- A printed list of references or reference letters
- A pen or pencil and a notebook
- A list of questions to ask the interviewer
- Your portfolio or any relevant papers or projects
- A copy of your transcripts
- A positive mental attitude

With the exception of the last item, which is absolutely mandatory, you may not need all of these items. But keep in mind that it is better to have them and not need them, than to need them and not have them. Use your judgment about which items are appropriate to take to each interview.

 What is appropriate attire for interviewing?

Now let's talk about attire. One of the very first things that interviewers notice when meeting applicants is their clothing. It is important to remember that while dressing appropriately may not guarantee that you will get the job, sloppy or inappropriate dress for an interview will just about guarantee that you will not get it. In deciding what clothes to wear to an interview, you should let common sense and the interview fashion tips in Figure 9.5 be your guide. These tips are meant to be a general guide, not an absolute dictum on what is appropriate in every situation. The guidelines are for the majority, but not all, of the professional, technical, and administrative jobs that most college graduates will apply for. There are exceptions to these guidelines. For example, someone interviewing for a position in the arts or entertainment fields, such as acting, modeling, or even fashion merchandising, probably would not want to follow these rules. This is where your common sense should come into play. If you are uncertain, ask someone who is familiar with the interview process. The counselors in your college or university career planning and placement office can help. Someone who is employed in the same field as the position for which you are interviewing could also give you some advice.

- For most professional-level jobs, the standard dark suit for both men and women is appropriate. For these type of jobs, conservative clothing is your best bet.
- Other, less formal, clothing such as a dark blazer and light colored trousers for men and a tailored dress for women may also be appropriate for certain professional jobs. Use common sense. Ask yourself "Would this be an appropriate outfit to wear if I were actually employed in this job?"
- Keep jewelry and cologne/aftershave to a minimum.
- When in doubt, it is better to err on the conservative side.

FIGURE 9.5
General Guidelines for Interview Attire

Arrival and Introductions

Now you are just about ready for the interview. As you prepare to leave for your appointment, keep in mind a rule that many recruiters and personnel managers adhere to: there is no excuse for being late to an interview. Always plan your trip so that you will arrive early by about 10 or 15 minutes. It does not make a favorable impression to arrive "fashionably late" for an employment interview. On the contrary, it will typically eliminate you from consideration. Arriving early will allow you time to relax and collect your thoughts prior to the meeting. Plan ahead for problems such as parking or getting lost. Realistically sometimes events beyond your control will cause you to be late, but to the greatest extent possible, you should plan for and minimize the number of things that could go wrong.

When you first meet the interviewer, introduce yourself, and offer a greeting such as "Mrs. Jones, I'm Bob Smith, how are you today?" A warm, friendly greeting is an excellent way to begin to create that all-important first impression. Always greet the interviewer by their surname (e.g., Mrs. Jones, Mr. Johnson) unless they tell you otherwise. Shake the interviewer's hand with a firm but not overpowering grip. This applies to men as well as women. In past years, proper etiquette dictated that a man did not shake a woman's hand unless she first extended hers. This is no longer the case. In the business world, it is perfectly acceptable to extend your hand in greeting when meeting someone, regardless of gender.

A few quick reminders are in order as the interview begins (see Figure 9.6). The first is to be aware of your posture when seated. When one is nervous, as often happens in an interview, there is a tendency to sit on the edge of the chair with both hands in the lap. This posture merely advertises one's nervousness and inhibits relaxation. During the interview you should sit comfortably, without slouching forward or leaning back too much. Do not cross your arms over your chest; this can convey a closed or defensive position.

The second reminder is to watch your grammar. What may be acceptable speech around your friends, may not be during an interview. Using poor grammar, double negatives, and other slang expressions can be costly. Employers do not want to hire people who have poor verbal skills. Conversely, it is also not a good idea to try and dazzle an interviewer by using a lot of flowery language. While a strong vocabulary is an asset, attempting to impress the interviewer by using big words, technical jargon, or otherwise overdoing it, is usually frowned upon.

Finally, be certain that you are making good eye contact with the interviewer. Many people find it unnerving to carry on a conversation with someone who will not look them in the eye. A common reason cited by interviewers for giving an applicant a low rating is a failure to make eye contact. Some studies have shown that people associate poor eye contact with a lack of trustworthiness, so pay particular attention to this aspect of your nonverbal communication.

Question and Answer Time

A good interviewer will typically, at this time, ask a question or make a comment that is unrelated to the interview, merely to break the ice and start the conversation on a light note in order to make you feel more relaxed and comfortable. After exchanging pleasantries, let

FIGURE 9.6
Things to Remember at the
Beginning of an Interview

- Arrive early
- Be cordial and friendly to the receptionist
- Fill out paperwork if asked
- Greet interviewer by name and with a smile
- Shake hands
- Thank interviewer for meeting with you
- Relax

the interviewer guide the discussion. Your role, at least for now, is to follow her lead, answer her questions, and ask questions when appropriate. Here is where all of your interviewing practice will pay off. If you have adequately prepared, these 30 minutes or so that you spend in the initial interview will go exceptionally well. You should be able to respond to her questions with good answers that highlight your strengths and demonstrate your qualifications for the position.

Remember that no matter how good a job you do preparing, you may still encounter the unexpected. For example, some interviewers will ask a "what would you do in this situation?" question. In using this technique, an interviewer will put you in a hypothetical scenario and ask you how you would handle it. The possible scenarios are endless and, as such, there is really no way to prepare for it, but you should be aware that you may run into this. When it happens, take a few moments to gather your thoughts and then give the best answer you can.

At the end of the interview, be sure to ask any questions you have that are still unanswered. It is perfectly acceptable to refer to the list of questions you made in your preparation for the interview. In all likelihood, many of these questions will be answered during the course of the interview.

As the interview winds up, if you are interested in the position, let the interviewer know. Do not leave her guessing as to whether or not you still want to pursue the job. A simple statement from you can help to accomplish this.

> I have enjoyed talking with you and I am very interested in the position.
> What is the next step in the interview process?

This accomplishes two things. First, you have let the interviewer know of your desire to pursue the job and, second, it will give you some idea of when you will hear from the organization on your status as a candidate.

The last thing you should do before leaving the interview is to thank the person or persons who interviewed you. They have taken time out of their day to talk with you and it is only fitting that you should express your gratitude. Interviewers, as with everyone else, like to be appreciated and by acknowledging their efforts, you leave a favorable impression of yourself in their minds (Figure 9.7).

After the Interview

After the interview, if you have not already done so, make a note of the name and title of the interviewers and be sure that you have their business mailing address. If you do not have this, ask a secretary, or if you are interviewing through the placement office at your school, ask one of the placement officials for this information. Within a day or two after the interview takes place, write a thank you note to each of the people with whom you spoke. Use the format outlined in chapter 8. This small gesture may make the difference as to whether or not you get called in for a second interview.

- Let the interviewer know if you are interested in the position
- Ask any unanswered questions
- Thank the interviewer
- Before you leave, make sure you have the name, address, and title of each interviewer
- Thank the receptionist

FIGURE 9.7
Things to Remember at the End of an Interview

Now comes the hard part—waiting. Most of the time what you are waiting for is not a job offer, but an invitation for a second interview. Most professional-level jobs require at least two interviews, although some companies require three or more. Some applicants get anxious and call the employer to find out the status of the job, but it is not wise to continually call the employer asking about where you stand and what your chances are of getting the job. A follow-up phone call may help your chances by letting the employer know that you are interested, but it may also backfire if you create a negative impression by pestering them. Generally speaking, patience is your best bet. Unfortunately there is no hard and fast rule to follow concerning how long to wait before calling if you have not heard from the employer. Use your best judgment.

If you are invited back for another meeting, it usually means that you are among a select few individuals who have passed the initial screening, and you deserve to pat yourself on the back because you have obviously done something right. The second interview usually consists of the applicant meeting the supervisors, department heads, corporate officers, etc. Depending on the organization's hiring policies, one might also expect to take personality tests, tour offices and plants, be taken out to lunch, etc. More specifics on job duties may be offered, and in all likelihood, if it has not yet been discussed, the compensation package will be disclosed.

EMPLOYER'S DECISION FACTORS

 What are the factors that will most quickly get you removed from consideration for a job?

There are many things that you can do during the course of an interview that will knock you out of contention for a job. Below is a short list of some of the negative factors that employers typically cite as inappropriate and which can remove you from consideration for a job.

- Poor appearance
- Lack of direction/goals
- No preparation for the interview
- Late for the interview
- What's-in-it-for-me attitude

These are just some of the mistakes applicants make. Be aware of these pitfalls and work to avoid them.

 What are the factors that employers look for during an interview that increase the applicant's odds of being hired?

Now that we have discussed the negative factors—things that you should avoid—let's take a brief look at some of the positive factors that employers look for in a prospective employee. The following represent attributes on which you will be evaluated during the interview process.

- Enthusiasm
- Knowledge of the employer and industry
- Campus involvement/leadership

- Neat, professional appearance
- Ability to communicate effectively
- Interest in the field of work
- Good academic record
- Evidence of teamwork/ability to work with others

These are general characteristics that employers look for when recruiting. Your job is to make sure that those aspects of your background which demonstrate these factors are evident to the employer during the interview. Become familiar with these attributes and be aware that interviewers are looking for them in their prospective employees. This will enable you to present yourself more effectively during the interview.

EVALUATING JOB OFFERS

 What factors should you consider when deciding whether or not to accept a job offer?

The job offer is the crowning event for the job hunter. It is a symbol of success and determination, creating a sense of pride in being selected over other applicants. It also raises an important question: "Should I accept this offer?" Or, if you have more than one: "Which of the offers, if any, should I accept?" There is a pervasive attitude among many job hunters to "go with the money" and while compensation is important, it should not be the only consideration when making a job choice. Several factors should go into your decision-making process, and adhering to a single-issue line of thinking can be counterproductive.

The major factors that should be considered when evaluating a job offer are basically the same for most people. What will vary is the degree of importance an individual places on each factor. Below is an outline of five of the major factors to be considered when deciding about a job offer and a brief synopsis of each element.

Duties/Nature of the Job

The overriding question you need to ask yourself when considering a job offer is "Would I enjoy this job?" If the answer is no, you need not go any further. Accepting a job that you know you would be unhappy with is a setup for dissatisfaction and failure. Except possibly in cases of financial exigency, you should never place yourself in the situation of going to work in a job you dislike. Be sure that you have a thorough understanding of all of the duties of the job including day-to-day activities, working hours, travel, necessary paperwork, supervision, etc., before making your decision.

Many times individuals are lured into a job with the promise of big money or prestige only to find that they are not cut out for the position and soon begin the job search process all over again. Others remain in a job for quite some time because of the money and later find themselves in a position of being unable to quit because they have become dependent on the level of income and cannot afford to start over in a lower paying job. This trapped feeling can result not only in dissatisfaction with the job, but can carry over and cause problems in one's personal life as well.

In short, a high level of interest in the nature and duties of a job should be a prerequisite for accepting a position. Overemphasis on money or "prestige" positions to the exclusion of other factors can lead to disaster.

Consistent with Personal Qualities

Early on in this text, we discussed self-assessment and its importance in the career decision-making process. Likewise, in job decision making you need to ask yourself if the position under consideration is consistent with your personal qualities. In other words, do your attributes mesh with those of the job? Of particular importance is an objective analysis of factors such as your values, motivations, abilities, etc. Will the job conflict with other aspects of your life that are important to you, such as spending time with your family? Are you willing to get up at 5:30 A.M. and work 10–12 hours per day if that is what the job requires? Will you pursue continued training in order to become proficient at the job? Are you willing to put in the time and effort required not to just get by, but to excel? The greater the degree to which the job is compatible with your personal qualities, the higher the probability of success in the position.

Advancement Potential

Be sure to take into consideration where the job could lead and what career opportunities await you if you accept the position. Consider things such as the employer's policy on promotions, where you could be in 5 years, 10 years, etc., and whether or not the job will allow you to accomplish your long-term goals. A dead-end job can be not only very frustrating, but detrimental to your career plans as well.

Location

Another factor for you to consider when evaluating a job offer is where you will have to live. Is the area appealing to you? Will you enjoy living there or just tolerate it for the sake of the job? How will the cost of living in that area affect the buying power of your salary? What about relocation costs—will you be responsible for this expense or will the employer pick up the tab? What moves will be required in the future? How long before you will be expected to relocate again? These are some of the questions that you will need to address and factor into your decision.

Compensation

The last aspect of job offer evaluation we will discuss is compensation. While in this text we have attempted to downplay the level of importance given to salary in both career and job offer decision making, let's face it, money is important. This does not mean that we have suddenly become greedy—on the contrary, we stick by our contention that it should not govern the choice process, but we accept that most people, given a choice, would prefer a higher income over a lower one.

In evaluating job offers you will need to consider not only the salary itself, but also what type of fringe benefits are offered (Figure 9.8). Always keep in mind that compensation is

FIGURE 9.8
Factors to Consider in
Compensation

- Salary
- Commissions
- Bonuses
- Vacation policy
- Health benefits
- Life insurance
- Company automobile
- Continuing education benefits
- Other perks

more than just salary. Benefits such as insurance, vacation policy, company automobile, and other perquisites can dramatically increase the value of a compensation package. Many times a low starting salary can be more than offset by a good benefits package. Be sure that this, in addition to the salary, is figured into your decision.

Salary Negotiation

 How should you handle the issue of compensation when it is brought up?

When it comes to the compensation package, different employers have different policies. Some have a standard starting salary for each position that is nonnegotiable. These employers make offers on a take it or leave it basis. Either you accept their compensation package or they offer it to someone else. If you are offered a position by one of these employers, you will have no success in trying to negotiate with them. If you feel as though you would like the job but that the pay is not at the level you want, or could afford to live on, let them know this and tell them what your salary requirements are. Be aware that, in doing so, you will probably price yourself out of the job.

Other employers will ask you for your salary requirements without revealing their range for the position. These employers are usually doing one of two things. They could be very interested in you and want to know what it would take for them to get you. Or they could be "fishing" to see how low a starting salary they can offer you and still keep your interest. Their rationale is why start someone off at $30,000 if they would accept $25,000? When an employer puts you on the spot by asking you what salary you require, what should you do? Two steps that you should take prior to interviewing will help you to handle this situation. To begin with, you should have some idea of what the typical starting salary is for that particular type of job. If you are unfamiliar with salary ranges, talk with a career counselor at your school prior to the interviewing process; he can give you this kind of information. Also salary surveys are available which provide similar data; check to see what resources are available on your campus. Second, you should have a good idea of what your financial needs will be. If you have not already done so, spend some time making a list of your anticipated living expenses after graduation and then decide what level of income you will need to meet those expenses.

Back to the question of how to handle this type of situation. You need to be careful because you do not want to price yourself out of contention by asking for an exorbitant salary, but you also do not want to work for peanuts when the employer is willing to pay you more. If the employer asks you for your requirements, it is best to try to avoid answering until you have some idea of their usual pay range for that position. Knowing this information will give you an idea of what salary figure or range you should present. Sometimes turning the question around and asking what is the typical starting salary for the position will get you the information you want. Other times it will not. If pressed for a dollar figure, give the interviewer a range with the low end being your desired (but realistic) salary expectations and the upper end being $3,000 to $4,000 more. At the same time, indicate that, naturally, you would like to make in the upper end of that range, but for the right position, you may consider less. This way, the low end of your range would be acceptable to you, but if the organization really wants you they may pay you more in an effort to persuade you to accept the job.

The Final Decision

The factors outlined above are not meant to be an exhaustive list of all the criteria to consider when evaluating a job offer. While these factors address most of the important considerations, there may be additional criteria that you feel are important when deciding whether or not to accept the job. Other factors could include the type of work environment (i.e., manufacturing versus service organization), proximity to family, climate, availability of recreational activities, or any number of other factors that you deem important. For some people the job either "just feels right" or it "doesn't feel right" and acceptance or rejection is made on that basis alone. Ultimately you should be the one to decide which guidelines and parameters to use in your decision-making process. Nobody knows better than you what is best for you, so make your decision with confidence. If you choose to accept the job, great; your job search is over, at least for now. If you decide to turn down the offer, have faith in your ability to choose wisely and allow yourself to feel good about the decision.

SUMMARY

Learning how to skillfully present yourself in an employment interview is one of the best methods for acquiring job offers. A strong background with excellent credentials does not assure an applicant of a job. An effective interview, on the other hand, especially when combined with good credentials, is a sure formula for finding yourself on the short list of top applicants for a job. Even a less than stellar background can be overcome by a strong interview.

There are several steps that you can take to polish up your interviewing skills. The key lies in preparation. Acquiring information ahead of time about the organization and the position will place you in an advantageous position when meeting with the interviewer. This, along with anticipating questions and developing possible answers, will help to ease some of the anxiety associated with the face-to-face interview. Participating in mock interviews and other practice techniques can help you hone your presentation skills and do a significantly better job during the interview, resulting in more job offers.

EXERCISES AND DISCUSSION QUESTIONS

1. Make a list of 10 interview questions that you feel a recruiter might ask you about your background and experience. Make a brief outline of the points you would want to make when answering these questions and practice them until you feel comfortable that you can effectively answer each. You may even want to participate in a mock interview in class, presenting your answers.

2. Choose an organization with whom you would like to interview for a professional-level position. Identify four or five informational sources that you can use in preparing for an interview. What specific information on the organization do you believe would be most helpful in your preparation?

3. Imagine that you are a recruiter for a large firm, interviewing recent college graduates for a position with your firm. Other than the specific skills and course work that are needed for the job, what are the *personal* characteristics you would be looking for in the applicants? After completing this list, objectively assess yourself with respect to these characteristics. How close are you to your "ideal" candidate?

4. Interviewing for the same position, which of these two individuals would you say has a better chance of being offered the job: someone who has a background that is exactly what the employer is looking for but possesses weak presentation skills, or someone who is somewhat less qualified but who has significantly stronger interviewing skills? Support your answer.

5. You have been called in for a second interview and have just been offered a great job that you are very excited about and were hoping to get. However, the offer is a few thousand dollars less than you wanted. What options do you have? How would you handle this situation?

10

Developing Job Search Strategies

After completing this chapter you should understand:

- *The various methods used in seeking employment*
- *How to most effectively market yourself to prospective employers*
- *Which job search methods provide the best chance for success*

INTRODUCTION

 How do I communicate my availability to those employers who are most likely to need my services?

Receiving a desirable job offer is a very exciting and rewarding event, especially if it is the culmination of years of study and preparation. The time spent in school, the effort exerted, the money spent, and the sacrifices made, finally all seem worthwhile. Each stage of the career development process covered thus far—self-assessment, career information, decision making, developing employability, and job readiness—has been a stepping stone on the road to finding that "perfect job" and becoming successfully employed. Recall from chapter 1 that this term means that you are productively employed in a position for which you have been educated and trained, which you find enjoyable, and which is consistent with your career goals. Learning where and how to locate those job openings that can lead you to successful employment is the focus of this chapter (Figure 10.1).

When job hunting, most people do not tap all of the resources available to them. Many job hunters limit their search to those positions listed in the help wanted section of the

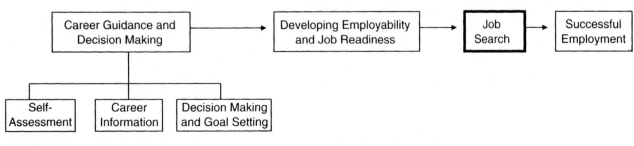

FIGURE 10.1
The Job Search

newspaper. Unfortunately for these people, they are missing out on most of the job openings for which they are qualified. Research shows that only about 15–20% of all job openings are ever published anywhere (Powell, 1990; Snelling, 1987), including newspapers, trade journals, and job listing publications. So those who rely on finding job listings by checking only these sources are missing out on up to 85% of the possible openings. Effective job searching is a structured, systematic process that employs varying approaches that maximize the likelihood of success. The remainder of this chapter is dedicated to identifying and illustrating those strategies that can be used to help ensure a successful job search.

JOB SEARCH STRATEGIES

There are several approaches that may be taken in facilitating the job search process. Each of the strategies presented in this chapter has inherent strengths and weaknesses. No one strategy will guarantee success, and your best bet is to adopt your own job search strategy using a combination of the ones outlined here.

Networking

Networking, as a job search strategy, is recognized as one of the best ways to uncover job leads and put yourself in a position to interview for a job. This strategy is rooted in the saying "It's not what you know, but who you know that counts." While this statement may seem cynical, and even unfair to some, it is actually the method by which most jobs are acquired in this country. Networking is a campaign of referrals whereby job hunters use contacts to help them search out leads and eventually make contact with those individuals within an organization who have the power to hire (Figure 10.2). In other words, the job seeker asks for employment information from acquaintances. The information sought should include not only specific job openings, but also referrals—names of other individuals who might be of assistance.

   Let us suppose that you decide to use this strategy in your job search. Who should you contact and what should you tell them? Your contacts should include anyone you believe could offer information about job openings in your field or who can refer you to someone else. You may want to make a "networking list" of people to contact. You should begin your list with people you know on a personal level, family, friends, and acquaintances.

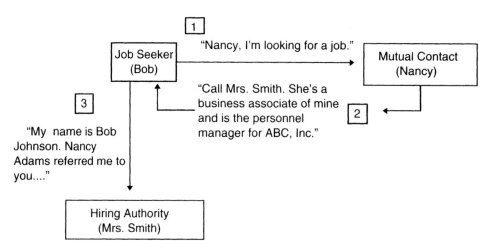

FIGURE 10.2
Networking Lines of Communication

Family includes not only your parents and siblings, but other relatives such as grandparents, aunts, uncles, etc. Friends of yours, and their parents, also make excellent contacts for job opening information. Friends of your family, such as business colleagues and social acquaintances of your parents, can also prove to be very helpful. Be sure to tap into these resource people; one of them may hold the key to your employment success.

Your networking list should also include former professors, supervisors, alumni, or anyone else who you feel could possibly help you. Place particular emphasis on people who are employed in or affiliated with an occupational field that is of interest to you. But even if you know someone who is not employed in a related field, it is a good idea to network with them as well, because they may know of someone who is in your field and could help you. It never hurts to ask.

It is important to remember that networking is a numbers game, meaning that the more contacts you make, the better your chances of success. Put out as many "feelers" as you can. What you will find is that most people are more than happy to help you. Most have been involved in their own job search before and understand the position you are in.

Because of the nature of the referral process, networking can drastically increase the number of contacts one is able to make. Let's assume that a job seeker tells two acquaintances that he is looking for a job. These two individuals probably meet and talk with dozens of other people in the course of their day. In turn, those people also make numerous contacts with other coworkers, friends, etc. In all of these contacts it is quite possible that the subject of job openings and hiring will come up, and when it does your name could be remembered and passed on.

The web effect of networking, as illustrated in Figure 10.3, shows how effective networking can be. Even using a conservative figure like two contacts per person per day, it does not take long for the number of contacts to become very large. After only the third level in the web, the two initial contacts have turned into 14. If the job seeker makes direct contact with 8 people, there would quickly be 56 contacts. And if he networks directly with 20 people . . . well, you see the power of networking.

Granted, everyone that you directly contact will not necessarily run out and tell others that you are looking for a job. However, as stated above, the probability that someone in the web will know of a job opening is very high. So don't be afraid or embarrassed to let others know that you are looking for a job. Talk it up. The more contacts you make, the more likely it is that you will find an outstanding opportunity. Use Exercise 10.1 to help you organize your networking list.

Here is what to tell your contacts when networking: (1) the type of job you are looking for, (2) your qualifications (education, work experience, etc.), (3) when you will be available for employment, and (4) contact information (telephone number, address). If the person is not a family member, or is unfamiliar with your background, it is a good idea to offer a copy of your resume so that they will have a better knowledge of your qualifications.

FIGURE 10.3
The Networking Web

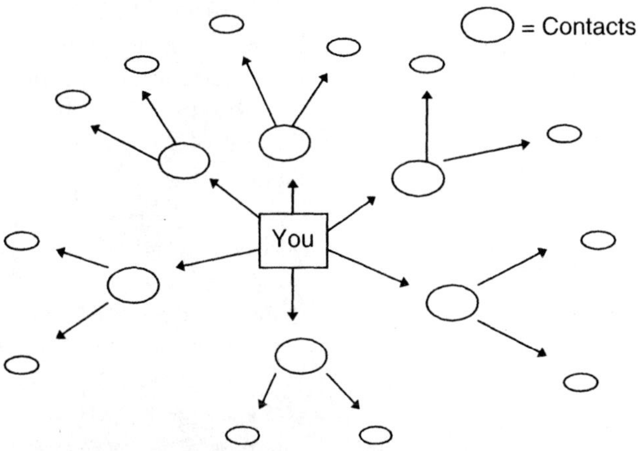

Do not offer any salary figures. If asked, tell the contact person that salary is not the main issue, that finding the right job is more important to you. The rationale behind not revealing your salary requirements is that if you tell someone that you want $28,000, he may not tell you when he hears of a job that pays only $26,000. It could be that that particular job would be very appealing to you and you would not be opposed to starting at a slightly lower salary. By the same token, an employer may be willing to pay $30,000 for the right person, but if the hiring authority knows that you have stated a lower figure, you could be losing money. You should be the one to decide whether or not to pursue a position, and by leaving your salary requirements negotiable, you will help ensure this.

Placement Services

The term *placement service* is a catch-all word for any organization which acts as an intermediary between people who are in the market for a job and employers. This includes college placement offices, state and federal employment offices, and private employment agencies. Here we will look at the different types of placement services that are available to job hunters.

Career Planning and Placement Office.   One of the most potentially profitable relationships you can develop during your college years is with your college career planning and placement office. Getting to know the counselors, and giving them the opportunity to get to know you, your background, and your career goals can pay off when you begin your job search process. These people are in direct contact with many organizations who hire recent college graduates and, no doubt, some of these employers hire people with your credentials every year. The more familiar the career counselor is with you, the better able he will be to steer you to the type of job openings that suit you.

If your placement office has an on-campus recruiting program, your career counselor can give you a listing of all of the employers who will be interviewing on campus. You can then choose those employers you are interested in and submit your resume for consideration. In addition to on-campus recruiting, college placement offices also have other job listings. Most keep current position announcements on file from companies who are hiring graduates. Since they may not send recruiters to your campus, you will have to contact them yourself, submit a resume if requested, and schedule an interview at their office. If the placement office has a resume referral service, you can have your resume and other application materials forwarded directly to the employer.

Individual placement offices may have additional sources of job listings such as monthly publications of public and private sector jobs, computerized job list databases, overseas employment opportunities, etc. Check with your placement office to find out what job lead sources are available to you.

State Employment Office.   State employment offices offer another resource for the job hunter. These agencies provide job listing and placement services to the public at no charge. As opposed to the college placement office, the positions listed with these agencies represent all levels of educational attainment and are not exclusively for those people with a college degree. Typically these agencies offer employment opportunities in a broad spectrum of occupational fields. Local job openings as well as computerized job listings that provide information on jobs in other areas can usually be found at this office. Check the telephone book for the location of the nearest state employment office and ask about their services.

Private Employment Services.   The last type of placement service that we will discuss is the private employment agency. These organizations operate much the same as the other placement services in that they put job seekers in touch with potential employers; however, they do so for a fee—sometimes a very expensive fee. It is common for these companies to specialize in one, or just a few, occupational areas. For example, one agency may find jobs for people in the engineering field, while another may focus exclusively on the medical profession. Some have placement specialists from several different fields in the same office. If you decide to use a private service, call them first and find out which occupational areas they specialize in.

If you accept a job through a private agency, a placement fee will be charged. The amount of the fee varies, but a common fee schedule used in the industry charges 1% for every $1,000 of the starting annual salary. In other words, placing someone in a $30,000 a year job would net a recruiting firm 30% of the first year salary, or $9,000. As a general rule, the employer will pay this fee, but in some cases the employee must pick up the tab. Be sure to ask about the fee policy *before* signing on with a recruiting firm.

Job Vacancy Listings

Most people, when they hear the term *job vacancy listing,* think of the help wanted section of the newspaper. While this is, indeed, an example of a job vacancy list, there are many other employment listing sources that are available to the job hunter. For example, most career fields have their own journals, magazines, and newsletters that contain articles concerning issues pertinent to that field. Many of these publications have a help wanted or job listing section as well. *Marketing News,* for instance, is a biweekly newsletter that has job openings in addition to articles related to the sales and marketing profession. Similarly, if you are interested in finding a job at a college or university, *The Chronicle of Higher Education,* a weekly newspaper geared toward this market, has hundreds of position announcements every week.

If it is a governmental position you want, there is the *Federal Employment Digest,* a monthly listing of federal government job opportunities. Also, most of the larger government agencies publish their own lists of positions that are available within their organization. By contacting the personnel departments of these agencies you can find out how to get their job vacancy lists.

In addition to printed job lists, there are also computerized job listing databases that provide innumerable job announcements in nearly every occupational field. The *Federal Job Information Computer* and *NationJob Network* are both examples of this type of computerized job vacancy listing. There are also numerous Web sites available on the Internet that provide job vacancy listings. These services can quickly put you in touch with a large number of position openings.

Be sure to ask someone in your school's career planning and placement office, career resource center, library, or local state employment service for more information on these and other types of job vacancy listings. In your job hunting it is important that you research as many as possible of these different resources. The more of these resources you use, the greater the likelihood that you will find just the right job.

Organizational Targeting

Each of the job search strategies that we have discussed thus far—networking, placement services, and job vacancy listings—generally approach the job search by identifying a *type* of job to look for. Accounting majors, for example, will naturally search under the Accounting job listings. And when networking with others, they tell them that they are looking for an accounting job. Clearly, this search strategy identifies the job type as the basis for the search.

There is another direction from which one can approach the job search, known as *organizational targeting.* Instead of focusing on a particular job type, this strategy looks at individual organizations as the basis for the search. Here job seekers identify, or "target," employers they would like to work for, and then contact them directly. The success rate with this method is lower because, unlike using vacancy lists or placement services, when contacting an employer, the applicant does not know whether an opening even exists. The advantage though is twofold: (1) you may locate jobs that are not otherwise known to the public, and (2) you get to choose the companies and organizations that you feel are best suited to your career interests and goals.

How should you conduct a campaign of organizational targeting? You begin by making a list of "targeted" organizations—those that you believe would have the most to offer you and which are likely to need the services of someone like yourself. Your library and/or career planning and placement office will have information on specific companies and organizations that you can use to develop your list. When making your list, keep in mind what it is that you are looking for in a potential employer. The purpose is to identify only the most promising organizations—the ones that you believe are the most likely to be able to offer you the opportunity for high levels of success and satisfaction. Exercise 10.2 provides a checklist to help you to gain a better picture of the type of companies or organizations that you feel are best suited for you. Completing it can help you identify prospective firms and add to your list of targeted organizations.

The next step in organizational targeting is to contact the employers you have targeted by writing a letter of inquiry (see chapter 8) and enclosing a resume. If at all possible, it is a good idea to find out the name of the person who would be responsible for hiring someone with your qualifications and direct the letter to her attention. You may want to follow up with a phone call and ask the hiring authority for an interview. Even if there is no opening available, ask that your resume be kept on file. This way, if a position becomes available in the future, the organization will already have your credentials on file and you will have the advantage of having already spoken to the hiring authority.

Using the Telephone.   A variation on the organizational targeting strategy is to make the initial contact with the employer by phone. Instead of sending a letter of inquiry, this approach advocates calling the organization and, if you do not have a name, ask to speak to the person who does the hiring in your occupational field. When you get that person, be direct and to the point. After the introduction, give a very brief synopsis (10–15 seconds, or so) of your background including a "teaser." A teaser is a selling point, some aspect of your background that would be appealing to a prospective employer. After this short sales pitch, ask the hiring authority if she foresees any job openings in your field in the near future. Here is an example of how one might conduct this type of contact with Ms. Robinson, Personnel Director of XYZ Corporation:

> Ms. Robinson, my name is Mary Ann Carter. I am a recent graduate of State University with a degree in Human Resources Management. As part of my degree requirements, I completed a summer internship with Acme Industries in their Employee Benefits department and I am now seeking permanent employment in a related field. I am familiar with XYZ Corporation and would like to ask if you anticipate any job openings in my field in the near future.

Here the job hunter has clearly stated the purpose of her call and offered a teaser—her related work experience. Remember to keep your presentation very short. Do not try to give a complete rundown of your qualifications; doing so will try the patience of the hiring authority—something you really do not want to do at this point.

If you find an organization that is hiring, ask questions about the position, and if it sounds like something you are interested in and qualified for, ask how to apply for the job. If the hiring authority says that she is not looking for anyone with your background, ask her if she knows of any other organizations which might hire someone like yourself. Be sure to send a thank you note for her time, along with your resume, and ask that you be considered for any future positions that come open in your field.

Even though you are taking a "shot in the dark" with the organizational targeting strategy, there is a distinct advantage to this method of job search. With this strategy, you are taking a more proactive approach to your job search. Instead of limiting your search only to job openings, you are going directly to those employers that you believe would provide the best opportunity for successful employment. This broadens the scope of employment possibilities and allows you better access to those job opportunities that are not published or listed. Your percentage of "strike outs" or "we're not hiring" responses will be higher using this technique because the odds are that most of the employers you contact will not be looking for someone like you. Do not let this dissuade you; all it takes is a single positive response from one of your targeted organizations in order to find yourself in the running for a great job.

Mass Mailings

Another approach to contacting employers to check on job openings is the mass mailing strategy. In this approach the job hunter attempts to contact as many employers as possible who might possibly hire someone with his background and experience. The difference between this strategy and organizational targeting is that, in mass mailing, the job hunter is not as concerned about narrowing the list of potential employers to a few "choice organizations," but focuses more on increasing the number of contacts made. Under this approach, job hunters may have little knowledge of an employer, but a resume and letter of inquiry is mailed anyway in an attempt to get their name in front of as many hiring authorities as possible.

The reality of this strategy is that it has a very low success rate. According to Richard Bolles (1995), this strategy has a 92% failure rate. In other words, only 8 out of 100 job hunters who use this method find a job as a result of it. Granted, these are pretty low odds but, on the positive side, you may be one of those people in that 8%. If nothing else, you should consider this strategy as just one more avenue for you to pursue in your search for the right job.

SUMMARY

Finding a job takes a lot of work. A good job search campaign can be a time-consuming, tedious, and expensive undertaking. The rewards, though, can be very high. Knowing where to look for the best job opportunities is not always easy. Many of the best positions are never published, therefore a thorough job search involves contacting people who can point you in the direction of the openings.

Networking, a strategy where a job hunter makes contact with acquaintances and referrals in an effort to find job openings, represents one of the most effective methods for locating job openings. Other strategies include using placement services and searching job vacancy listings. Finally, "cold calling" techniques, such as organizational targeting and mass mailing, offer additional methods for locating job openings.

EXERCISES AND DISCUSSION QUESTIONS

1. Assume that you have just moved to a new town and do not know anyone there. What steps would you take to find employment? Who would you contact? What resources would you use to help you find a job?

2. "It's not what you know, but who you know that counts." This statement is often used in reference to job searching. How much validity do you think there is to this statement? Is there anything wrong with taking advantage of your contacts with family, friends, and acquaintances and having them "pull strings" to help you locate job leads and get interviews?

3. Do some research on your own into how people acquire jobs. Ask 10 people who are currently employed how they learned of and were hired for their jobs. Ask them also about previous jobs that they have had, and which job search techniques proved most successful. Do you see any patterns about how people find jobs?

4. Locate as many resources for job openings as you can find that are available on your campus (i.e., job posting boards, computerized job vacancy systems, etc.). Try to find some that are specific to your occupational area. Next, do the same thing for off-campus resources.

5. As a practice activity, make a list of 10 employers you would like to work for after graduation. Then find the name of the contact person within each organization who can provide you with information on job openings in your field. Try to get a specific name, address, and phone number. Later, when you begin your job search, you can use this technique to add to your list of contacts.

Exercise 10.1   Networking list

Make a list of people you know, or know of, who could possibly offer information that would assist you in your job search. Include family, friends, friends of family, family of friends, professors, advisors, supervisors, alumni, or anyone else who you believe could be of assistance.

	Name	*Phone*	*Date* *Contacted*	*Outcome* *(job opening, referral, etc.)*
1.				
2.				
3.				
4.				
5.				
6.				
7.				
8.				
9.				
10.				
11.				
12.				
13.				
14.				
15.				
16.				

Make duplicates of this page as needed.

Exercise 10.2   Preferred Employer Characteristics

Place a check next to each of the characteristics that describe the type of company or organization you would most like to work for. Use the resulting profile to help you identify prospective firms for targeting in your job search.

Size of Organization

☐ Large (5,000 employees)   ☐ Medium (500–4,999 employees)

☐ Small (499 or fewer employees)   ☐ No preference

Type of Industry

☐ Accounting   ☐ Hotel and Lodging

☐ Agriculture   ☐ Law

☐ Architecture   ☐ Law Enforcement

☐ Communication   ☐ Manufacturing

☐ Computers   ☐ Mining

☐ Construction   ☐ Publishing

☐ Education   ☐ Restaurant

☐ Engineering   ☐ Sales, financial

☐ Entertainment   ☐ Sales, retail

☐ Forestry   ☐ Sales, wholesale

☐ Government   ☐ Transportation

☐ Health Care   ☐ Travel

☐ Other_____   ☐ Other_____

Geographic Location

☐ Large city   ☐ Northeast U.S.   ☐ Specific states   _____

☐ Medium city   ☐ Southeast U.S.   _____

☐ Small town   ☐ Midwest U.S.   _____

☐ Rural   ☐ Southwestern U.S.   ☐ Foreign countries _____

                   ☐ Northern U.S.   _____

Interpretation

Use the information in this exercise to help you gain a better understanding of what it is that you desire in a prospective employer. Then use this insight to begin the process of identifying organizations that would meet your criteria for an ideal working environment.

Maintaining Productivity and Employability

After completing this chapter you should understand

- *How to ease the school-to-work transition*
- *What major factors contribute to success on the job*
- *How to develop a "success mentality"*
- *How the career development model can be used as a lifelong guide for ensuring successful employment and career satisfaction*
- *The importance of establishing a balance between work and home life*

INTRODUCTION

 What steps can you take to help ensure continued success in your career?

It finally happened. The payoff from all those years of school has arrived. You have just received a great offer from a terrific firm and your professional career has begun (Figure 11.1). Your focus will now switch from achieving academic success to ensuring a successful and rewarding professional career. Achievement and recognition in your career will require effective job performance. You will be faced with many new challenges and opportunities to prove your worth, and how you handle these situations will determine your degree of success or failure. There are many factors that contribute to success on the job, and it is important to familiarize yourself with these concepts and to plan for success in your career. This chapter outlines those factors which have been demonstrated to lead to job success.

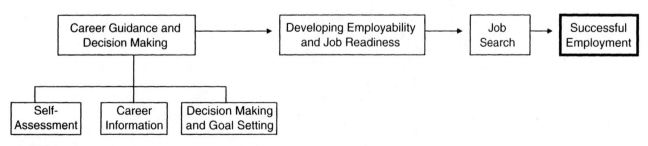

FIGURE 11.1
Successful Employment

Before we turn our attention to these success factors, there is an important point to be made about this period in your life. You need to understand that making the switch from college student to full-time employee is a big adjustment. Many of the things that you did as a student, such as skipping 8:00 classes in order to sleep late or scheduling your classes so that your afternoons are free, are no longer options. You will be expected to work 40 hours or more per week, endure a drastic reduction in your free time, and adhere to a much more rigid schedule than you have been used to. Initially, it may be difficult to adjust to these changes.

You also need to remember that just because you are out of school, you are not through learning. As you begin your first job, you will probably have to go through a training program where you are once again a student. The difference is that during this training process it is no longer your grades that will suffer in the event of poor performance, but your career.

On the flip side, there are many positive aspects to beginning your career. With your newly acquired income, you will be able to afford things that you have previously been unable to buy. A new car, new wardrobe, money for travel, and possibly even a house are a few of the benefits of your new career. The luxuries that you forfeited in order to obtain your degree are now within reach. Enjoy them—you've earned them.

There are many other changes and adjustments during this time. Personal responsibility, for example, becomes evermore critical and, for some, facing this can be a difficult transition. How well you handle this period of change will determine the degree to which your career gets off to a successful start. Be especially aware of the changes going on within and around you during this period in your life. Your success may depend on it.

JOB SUCCESS FACTORS

 What factors contribute most to job and career success?

As we noted earlier, a successful career requires effective job performance. Implicit in this idea of effective job performance is the notion that there are certain traits associated with superior workers. These are characteristics that most employers look for and reward in their employees. In Figure 11.2, we have arranged a few of the most important of these traits into a group, which we call *job success factors*. As you read through this section, keep in mind that these are characteristics associated with successful employees—those who excel—and find ways to develop these traits and include them in your work habits.

Attitude

Karin Ireland, in *The Job Survival Instruction Book* (1994, p. 7), advises that "The three most important parts of your job performance are attitude, attitude, and attitude." One of the most important things that you should be aware of as you enter the workforce is that your attitude toward your work, employer, and coworkers will play a significant role in your success or failure on the job. In fact, studies have shown that attitude and related personality traits are more important than skills or knowledge in effecting promotions, and that job failure is more frequently due to poor human relations, not a lack of skills (Steele & Morgan, 1991). Nobody wants to work with someone who has a disagreeable disposition, who complains and bad-mouths, or who is insensitive to the thoughts and feelings of others. These people are usually overlooked by management as candidates for promotions due to their negative attitude.

On the other hand, and not surprisingly, those workers who are best received and most likely to enjoy advancement are those who possess a positive attitude, good interpersonal skills, and a friendly, courteous demeanor. As you enter the work world, take an honest, objective look at yourself and see if there is room for improvement in these areas.

Teamwork

A study of almost every successful organization reveals a characteristic common to each: the ability of its employees to work as a team. Pulling together to achieve common goals is an important aspect of any successful organization, and as part of the team you will need to be able to demonstrate a high level of teamwork skills. This means not only completing tasks assigned to you, but helping fellow employees when needed. As team members, their success is your success and vice versa. By working together, obstacles can be overcome and the team can achieve success that would be unattainable working independently.

FIGURE 11.2
Job Success Factors

Attitude

Teamwork

Fitting In

Initiative/Follow Through

Accepting Guidance and Criticism

Keeping Current

Problem Solving/Decision Making

Professionalism

A good team member is one who is willing to listen to opposing points of view with an open mind. He possesses a high degree of respect and tact in dealing with coworkers, especially when faced with areas of disagreement. A willingness to compromise when needed is also a characteristic of the successful team member. These qualities, while not always easy to display, are necessary for becoming a productive member of an organization.

Fitting In

Closely related to the idea of teamwork is the ability of an employee to "fit in" with coworkers by following organizational customs. One of the quickest ways for a new employee to alienate himself from his fellow employees is to adopt an "I'm going to do things my way" attitude. There are many unwritten rules in the workplace, meaning that there are certain things that you will be expected to do, or not do, that are not part of the organization's formal rules and regulations. For example, some offices have an understanding among the employees that certain errands or chores will be alternated between themselves. Making coffee, going to the post office, picking up supplies, sharing overtime duties, etc., are examples of this type of unwritten agreement. If you, as a new employee, refuse to share in these duties because "it's not my job," you run the risk of being ostracized by the other employees. This can make for a very unpleasant work situation and prevent you from being accepted as part of the team. Rest assured that this rejection by your coworkers will not go unnoticed by supervisors. By not trying to fit in, you run the risk of becoming a social outcast, and can reduce or even eliminate the possibility of achieving success with that firm.

Abiding by organizational customs is difficult for some individuals. They are averse to the idea of following the expectations of others and do not want to conform. However, as a newcomer to an organization, bucking the system is usually counterproductive. The rules and norms have typically been around long before the new employee showed up, and will be there long after he is gone.

Even seemingly insignificant breeches of organizational protocol can land a worker in hot water. One newly hired employee made the mistake during his first staff meeting of taking a seat in a particular chair, which for years had been "reserved" for one of the long-time employees. The new worker was sternly informed by a coworker to "get up or get out!" Even a small infraction like this can cause resentment.

As you begin a new job, you will soon find out what, if any, unwritten rules exist. It behooves you to try and "fit in" by respecting these norms of behavior, and if you find that you cannot, it may be necessary to seek other employment. The inability to get along with coworkers is one of the most often-cited reasons given for employment termination. So make sure, when you begin a new job, that you make an extra effort to fit in with coworkers and follow the accepted standards of behavior.

Initiative/Follow Through

Demonstrating initiative in the workplace is not only a desirable characteristic in an employee, but is well recognized as mandatory for advancement. Initiative means exhibiting drive and motivation by undertaking tasks and projects that contribute to the success of the organization. It means contributing more than just what is expected by going above and beyond the minimum requirements of the job. It means asking for responsibility. It means completing tasks as efficiently as possible and on time.

By accepting responsibility and showing that you are capable of doing the assigned work and more, you are creating an impression in the minds of your supervisors that you are a dedicated, hard-working, reliable employee. The contribution that this image can have to your success should be obvious.

Accepting Guidance and Criticism

As you learn the ropes of your new job, it is important that you be able to accept help and guidance, as well as criticism, from others. These are qualities that will benefit you for your entire career. No matter how long you have been doing your job, or how proficient you become at it, there will always be room for improvement. Especially in the early stages of a job, you should not only accept guidance from those more knowledgeable and experienced, you should seek it out. Some individuals have a problem with what in their perception is "being told what to do." The reality is that, in the early stages of most jobs, you will be given instructions on what is expected of you and how to do it. This is always part of the formal or informal training program and it should not be perceived negatively.

Accepting criticism is not easy for many of us. Even when it is constructive criticism, we often bristle at being chastised. Mistakes are going to happen. Your supervisors know and accept this. What they do not accept is someone who shifts responsibility for their mistakes by making excuses and scapegoating. When you make a mistake, admit your responsibility without becoming defensive, and look on it as a learning opportunity. You will gain more respect from you supervisors and fellow workers by accepting responsibility than by making excuses for your mistakes.

The guidance and constructive criticism offered by superiors and coworkers is all part of the learning process. In most cases, the person doing the reprimanding is merely doing her job and is offering constructive criticism in order to help you do your job better. Accept it and learn from it.

Keeping Current

Keeping current means taking steps to continue to develop your knowledge and skills in your chosen field. Staying abreast of the recent trends and current issues allows you to stay up to date on important changes and new information in your occupational area.

This is especially true in the fields of technology and information processing. Almost every aspect of work has been touched by the explosion of computerization and other technological advances. These improvements require you to keep up with how technology is changing your work environment and to adapt accordingly or run the risk of watching your employable skills become obsolete. The field of drafting and architectural design, for example, is vastly different from what it was 15 years ago. Work that used to be done by several draftspersons using conventional, manual practices is today done by one person using sophisticated computer software. Those who have not adapted to the new technology have found themselves left behind.

Further advances will cause today's state-of-the-art technology to become outdated in just a few years, requiring continuing education and training on the part of employees in order to remain competitive in the workforce. Continued success in your chosen field of work will require you to keep current with procedural and technological advances.

Problem Solving/Decision Making

One changing aspect of workplace management in this country is that more and more firms are adopting a system of decentralized decision making. Employees at lower levels now have more responsibility for deciding on and implementing a course of action in a given situation, without having to get approval from higher-level management personnel. This means that more responsibility than ever before is being placed on entry- and lower-level personnel, and a premium is being placed on one's ability to make good, sound decisions.

Along with this decision-making authority, problem-solving ability becomes increasingly important. Problem-solving requires you to be able to identify the problem, develop alternative solutions, choose the best option, and implement the decision. The better your problem-solving skills, the better your decisions, and the better your chances for positive recognition and rewards.

Your problem-solving skills can be developed and improved. If you feel that this is a weak area for you, you should take steps to overcome this deficiency. There are numerous books that can offer assistance in this area, and even college courses and seminars that are designed specifically to help develop problem-solving and decision-making skills. Find out what resources are available to you and take advantage of them if needed.

Professionalism

The concept of professionalism is somewhat abstract and can mean different things to different people, but it generally refers to the expectation that an employee will adhere to a high level of ethical behavior and portray an image that is consistent with the organization's norms (Figure 11.3). While professionalism may not be easy to define, unprofessional behavior is glaringly obvious.

A common example is abuse of company time. This includes arriving late to work, taking too many coffee breaks and extended lunches, and leaving early. In addition, too much socializing, gossiping at the water cooler, and too many personal phone calls are also activities that can get you labeled as unprofessional.

Another aspect of professionalism that you need to be aware of is personal appearance. The clothes you wear and how you look will determine whether or not you portray a professional image to others. Make sure that your clothes are neat, clean, and not out of date, and be sure to emphasize personal hygiene. Unkempt and unclean are characteristics that you do not want associated with you. Your image plays a part in determining whether or not you advance within an organization, so make sure that you look the part.

FIGURE 11.3
Twenty Tips for Getting Promoted and Advancing Your Career

1. Arrive early to work
2. Dress appropriately
3. Find a mentor
4. Help out coworkers
5. Take on extra duties
6. Complete tasks/projects on time
7. Stay current in your field
8. Don't be afraid to make decisions
9. Give credit to coworkers when appropriate
10. Accept responsibility for mistakes
11. Ask for feedback from supervisors on your performance
12. Know what is expected of you
13. Act professionally
14. Respect organizational norms
15. Don't be a clock watcher
16. Keep personal business out of the office
17. Don't gossip
18. Set high goals
19. Be a pleasure to work with
20. Minimize complaining

There are so many other aspects to the concept of professionalism that we cannot cover them all. So much of what we say and do is a reflection of our degree of professionalism. Never forget, though, that professionalism means maintaining high ethical standards and work habits, and portraying a polished image. Employers look for these characteristics in their employees and exhibiting them can have a positive effect on your chances for advancement.

DEVELOP A SUCCESS MENTALITY

In addition to understanding and incorporating the job success factors into one's work, it has been suggested that using visualization can help facilitate career advancement and goal attainment. Richard Koonce, vice president of the regional office of EnterChange, an outplacement and career consulting firm, suggests that seeing yourself in a certain way and acting accordingly can do wonders for your career. In a recent article he writes that in order to help clarify what you want from your career and keep you on track, there are several things that you should get in the habit of doing on a regular basis. Below is a synopsis of his recommendations (Koonce, 1995). These mental exercises and associated actions can keep you in the right frame of mind and help to ensure your career success.

FOURTEEN WAYS TO NURTURE YOUR CAREER[1]

1. Realize that you are entitled to any job or career for which you are willing to strive and work. It may require some work, additional education, or patience. But if you've got gumption and stick-to-itiveness, you can accomplish just about anything you want. One of the most important keys to motivation is feeling you're worthy of something better. Don't ever affirm self-limitations!

2. Visualize yourself today in the job of your dreams. Focus at least 20 minutes of energy and effort every day on making that dream become a reality. You might want to write down your dream and put it on your refrigerator, on your bathroom mirror, or on the wall in your office. Seeing it each day will help you internalize its message and will help you move toward it.

3. Develop a strategy—solid and clearly stated steps that will help you move toward the job or career of your dreams. What career or careers do you want, and what reasonable, short-term goals will get you there? Developing strong career goals is the critical underpinning for taking charge of your career. Once you've developed goals for yourself, focus on moving toward them at least a little each day. Over time, taking small steps toward your goals is what leads to real success and the attainment of personal and professional objectives.

4. If you're not sure of exactly what you want next out of your career, give yourself permission to explore some options. For advice and help, seek out people you know and trust. Have faith that in doing so, you will move toward greater awareness of what you want for yourself.

5. Use your current circumstances as a springboard to something better. If you're not happy where you are, devise a plan of escape to move on to something else. Power up your professional contact network, update your resume, and go on informational interviews. Tap into the knowledge of friends and colleagues to help you define your job and career goals. Entertain the idea of doing something on an interim basis, to help you get your feet wet in a new professional arena, to stabilize your expenses, or buy time as you explore new career options. Have confidence that, in doing these things, you will be able to find a "back door" into a new job or to "cocreate" a new job for yourself with a new (or even your current) employer.

[1]From "Becoming Your Own Career Coach" by Richard Koonce, 1995, *Training and Development, 49,* p. 18. Copyright January 1995, *Training and Development,* American Society for Training and Development. Reprinted with permission. All rights reserved.

6. Develop an intense desire to achieve your career goals, and take note of defining moments or rites of passage that represent significant steps toward those goals. As your career progresses, you may complete a graduate degree, or give a speech, or write an article or a book, or otherwise complete some professional task that gives you a new or reinvigorated sense of self-confidence and professional purpose. Identify, savor, and celebrate moments of success like these—even if nobody in your organization notices them. They are mile markers for you on the way to your long-term career goals and dreams.

7. Realize that you are unique both as an individual and as a professional. You have a right to a meaningful job and career. In this regard, what you think of yourself is the key to your success and happiness. As Harvard psychologist William James once said, "You are what you think about most of the time!"

8. Don't let anybody tell you what you can and can't have out of a career! Some people will question your motives, your dreams, your chances, your intelligence, and your competence to do any job. This frequently happens to women and minorities, but it can happen to anyone. If it does, don't let it rattle you. It may be that they are envious of your dreams and impressed by (or threatened by or jealous of) your drive and intelligence. Indeed, as many capable women will attest, a lot of men are threatened by the competence of women.

Don't despair. Instead, take note of what Eleanor Roosevelt once said about facing adversity: "I gain strength, courage, and confidence by every experience in which I must stop and look fear in the face. I say to myself, 'I've lived through this and can take the next thing that comes along.' We must do the things we think we cannot do."

9. Strive to develop a professional identity that is independent of your current job description, title, and organization. Why? It's an unfortunate fact of professional life that most organizations tend to put their employees "in boxes," confining them and preventing them from using all of their skills and talents. At its worst, this can be dehumanizing. At the very least, it can be disempowering—if you buy into being put in a box.

There are a lot of ways to break out of the box—to develop a professional identity that is apart from and independent of your job title, position, or function in your organization. Consider getting involved in professional groups and associations. Develop a contact network that involves you with peers from other companies and organizations. Strive to become known in your field by presenting seminars and workshops and delivering talks to outside groups.

All of these activities outside your office will give you a sense of satisfaction, empowerment, self-confidence, and professional competence. Such experiences can be valuable to you at any point in your career, but they may be particularly useful if you are laid off or downsized. At times like that, you'll need sources other than your job from which to derive your professional identity—at least temporarily.

10. Don't rely on your boss or organization to define your career path or options, or even to understand what you do. Years ago, especially in large companies, mentoring employees was a standard part of a supervisor's job description. Today, things are quite different.

Organizations of all sizes and in all industries are dealing with change as they've never had to before, and managers spend most of their time managing bottom-line business objectives. They frequently have little time to worry about helping subordinates develop in their own careers. And in many cases, supervisors aren't comfortable with their ability to mentor others. You might have a terrific supervisor who is interested in helping you advance. But it isn't absolutely necessary to your job and career success.

11. Don't let yourself become a victim in your job or career. The victim mentality has gained a lot of currency in our culture in recent years. Of course, some people really are victims. But taking on the role of victim will not empower you to find or create better professional circumstances. It is far more likely to sap your energy and delay your entry into professional arenas that might be more rewarding than your current position.

12. Come up with some affirmations to sustain you as you go forward in your current job or as you make plans to change jobs or careers. Write an affirmation on a three-by-five card each day. Post it in a prominent place at home, in the office, or in your car, where you can be reminded of it and commit it to memory.

13. Commit yourself to continuous and lifelong learning. The reasons to be a lifelong learner should certainly be clear. To remain marketable in today's knowledge-based economy, you need to commit yourself to continuous learning throughout your career if you want to avoid becoming a professional dinosaur. Equally important is enjoying how you learn—whether you learn through reading, interacting with a new computer program, talking to other people, attending and presenting programs at conferences, or indulging in a little "intellectual grazing" from time to time at your favorite bookstore.

Which learning avenues appeal to you? Which represent a good fit with your personality, interests, and temperament? Find some and indulge in them. If you love the ways you learn, you will pursue learning with a passion all your life. You will not view learning as work or as education. You will see it as pleasure, even as recreation.

14. Be intentional and purposeful about taking charge of your professional life. It's important that you develop "intentionality" and presence of mind about where you want to go in the years ahead. This will open up your heart and mind to possibilities and options that you might not otherwise imagine.

At the same time, savor each day as much as you can, and find something—anything—about your daily work that you can enjoy or learn from. Even in the midst of difficulties, you may find omens that point you in new and more satisfying directions. As Napoleon Hill, the author and motivational expert, once advised, "Every adversity carries with it the seed of an equivalent or greater benefit." Thinking along the same lines was George Bernard Shaw, who wrote, "The people who get on in this world are those who get up and look for the circumstances they want, and if they can't find them, they make them."

CONTINUAL EVALUATION: KEY TO CAREER SUCCESS AND SATISFACTION

At the beginning of this book, in a quote from Donald Super, it was noted that a person's level of job satisfaction can change with time, and a job that was at one time very satisfying, may no longer be so today. An important implication of this is that your career development process is a never-ending cycle. Successful employment, as the desired outcome of the career development model, requires that from time to time you evaluate your overall career satisfaction.

In this ongoing evaluation the concept of goals, once again, becomes an important issue. Chapter 5 covered the necessity of goal setting in career success, and as you progress through your professional life, it is important that you always be aware of where you are in relation to your goals. From time to time you should review your current work situation and see if you are on track toward accomplishing your objectives. What was at one time important to you may not be so any more, and a realignment of your goals might be in order. Or it could be that you have gotten off course in pursuing your goals and need to navigate your way back on course. As you begin your career, you should once again complete Exercise 5.2, Career Goal Setting and Planning, and reassess your career objectives. Periodically thereafter pull it out and identify where you are in relation to where you want to be. Doing so will allow you to keep a sharp focus on what you want to accomplish and the steps necessary to get there.

If you are happy with your job and feel like you are achieving your objectives, great. Count your blessings and continue to work toward your goals. If, however, you find that you are not satisfied, feel hindered in your progress, or for some other reason you dislike what you are doing, you should ask yourself these questions:

1. "What is it about my job that I don't like?" Try to be as specific as you can about where the problem exists. Gain an understanding of whether the problem lies in the type of work you do, the organization you work for, the people you work with, lack of promotions, or another aspect of your employment. Spotlighting the problem will help you to come up with possible solutions.

2. "Can I change that aspect of my job?" After you have determined where the problem lies, look to see if it is possible to change that part of your job so that it is no longer a hindrance. If you dislike your job because of the commuting required in order to get to work every day, see if it is possible for you to move closer to your work. If it is the amount of paperwork that is required in your job that bothers you, look into the possibility of computerizing or otherwise reducing the amount of time spent on this duty. Look for solutions to the specific problem areas before you give up on the job as a whole.

3. "Will it get better?" Some of the negative aspects of a job will change as time goes by and you may not have to put up with them forever. Knowing that unpleasant duties are only temporary can help you to endure them until they are eliminated. Say, for example, you begin work with a national company which requires you to travel extensively—something you hate to do. It may be worth your while to stay in the position if you know that after the first year, you will probably be promoted to a position that requires little or no travel.

If you are not advancing within the organization, and feel that you should be, try to find out why. Is it your job performance? It is because your boss does not like you? Talk to your supervisor. It could be that they have future plans for your advancement that have not yet come to fruition. This information will certainly help you with evaluating your career position and options.

If you find that the answer to questions 2 and 3 is no, then you should seriously consider changing jobs. Your work should not be something that you have to do eight hours per day, five days per week, even though you hate it, just so you can pay your bills. It should be something you enjoy and look forward to. If you are unhappy and see no possibility of improvement, you need to make a change. Look again at what it is that you do not like about your job. It is the organization? If so, a change of employer may help. Is it the nature of the duties of the field you are in that bother you? Then another line of work may be necessary. Do you resent working hard to make a lot of money for someone else? You might consider entrepreneurship. By pinpointing the source of your unhappiness, you will be better able to decide the best course of action.

The usefulness of the career development model is reflected in its cyclical nature. As illustrated in Figure 11.4, the structure of the model allows you to return to the appropriate stage and use the guidelines presented to place your career back on the road to satisfaction and success. The point at which you reenter the model is determined by the nature of the dissatisfaction. For example, if you feel that you are in the wrong occupation, but do not know in which vocation you would be happiest, a return to the career guidance and decision-making stage would be in order. If, on the other hand, you enjoy the type of work that you do, but are discontented with your employer, it would be appropriate for you to return to the job search stage and use the techniques there to assist you in locating another job.

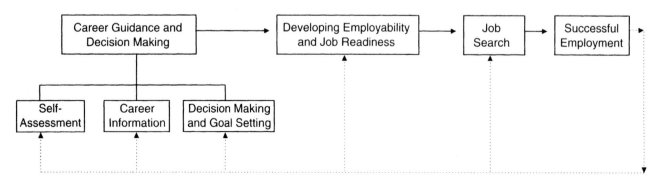

FIGURE 11.4
Cyclical Nature of the Career Development Model

For you, the ultimate objective of the career development model is to find employment in a job that you love and that allows you to achieve your career and personal goals. Life is too short and too precious to be unhappy. Since your career contributes so much to your overall level of happiness, it is vitally important that you find satisfaction in your work.

KEEPING A BALANCE

One final point about ensuring success and making your career as rewarding and fulfilling as possible: strive to find a balance between your work and your personal life. While working hard can contribute to your success, working too hard can have very negative consequences. Stress, burnout, job dissatisfaction, and other emotional problems are directly linked to an overemphasis on work. In addition, physical problems such as fatigue and ulcers can manifest themselves as symptoms of overwork. To modify a popular saying, "All work and no play makes Jack an unhealthy boy."

The importance of your personal life, spending time doing things away from work, cannot be over emphasized. The fun and enjoyment that you receive from spending time with family and friends and engaging in your favorite leisure activities has a balancing effect on your working life. A diversion from focusing on your work for eight or more hours per day is needed to prevent job burnout and other unwanted consequences. Even though you like your job, it is wise to spend time doing other things that you enjoy, away from the workplace, and avoid getting into a "rut."

Many people adopt the attitude that they will work hard and save money, forsaking luxuries such as fun and recreation until they retire, and then reap the rewards of all of those years of dedication. These are those "workaholics" who put in 14-hour days, rarely, if ever, take vacations, and do not engage in leisure or fun activities, preferring to spend their time in career-advancing activities. The problem with this "job first, enjoy later" mentality is that factors beyond their control may keep these individuals from enjoying their planned-for retirement. Illness, financial catastrophe, or many other events may prevent them from engaging in the activities that they had hoped and worked for. Recognizing that dedication is one of the job success factors we discussed, and an admirable quality, it must also be weighed against the negative factors mentioned above—burnout, stress, etc. While planning ahead for your retirement years is important and recommended, it is also important to look at today and find a healthy balance between doing your job and engaging in rewarding activities outside of work. Hobbies, exercise, recreational activities, religious interests, etc., can help you to keep your "balance" and elevate your career and personal happiness.

SUMMARY

The eight job success factors outlined in this chapter are the fundamentals for achieving recognition and success in your job as well as your career. Make it a practice to continually evaluate yourself in these areas to see if you are where you need to be, or if there is room for improvement. Your ability to assess, and redirect if necessary, your performance in these areas will determine your level of achievement on the job.

Developing a success mentality is another recommended method for career achievement and satisfaction. This involves visualizing success and using self-affirmations to keep yourself in a positive frame of mind. It also means not allowing others to dictate what you can and can't have from your career. Personal initiative, developing objectives, and taking small steps each day toward obtaining your goals are fundamental requirements for true success.

Finally, striving toward finding a balance between work and home life can actually help to ensure career success. Overemphasis on work can result in burnout and dissatisfaction. Spending time engaging in leisure activities can recharge your batteries and give you a renewed, refreshed, healthy perspective when returning to work. This positive mental attitude, when carried over into the job, can make work more satisfying and productive, and help to ensure career satisfaction.

EXERCISES AND DISCUSSION QUESTIONS

1. Review the job success factors listed in this chapter. Which ones are areas of strength for you? How can you use these to your advantage? Which ones are areas of weakness? How can you improve your weak areas?
2. What is the relationship between lifelong learning and career success? Can you have one without the other? Support your answer.
3. Write a career plan. Indicate where you would like to be in one year. Five years. Ten years. Twenty years. Include information on the types of jobs you would like to have, where you will live, your income, etc. What will you have to sacrifice in order to achieve these goals? How does the term "career navigation" (from chapter 5) apply to your goals?
4. Play the role of a career counselor. Someone comes to you who is unhappy with their job. He has been in the workforce for 10 years and is experiencing burnout. He complains about disliking his job, but does not know what to do about it. How would you help this person? What recommendations would you offer?
5. Define career success from your perspective. What circumstances would have to exist in order for you to be able to say you have a successful career?

References

Chapter 1

Brown, D., Brooks, L., & Associates (1990). *Career choice and development: Applying contemporary theories to practice* (2nd ed.). San Francisco: Jossey-Bass.

Gordon, V. N. (1981). The undecided student: A developmental perspective. *Personnel and Guidance Journal, 59,* 433–439.

Herr, E. L., & Cramer, S. H. (1991). *Career guidance and counseling through the life span* (2nd ed.). Boston: Little, Brown.

Isaacson, L. E., & Brown, D. (1993). *Career information, career counseling, and career development* (5th ed.). Boston: Allyn and Bacon.

Tolbert, E. L. (1982). *An introduction to guidance: The professional counselor* (2nd ed.). Boston: Little, Brown.

Chapter 2

Bloch, F. E. (1994). *Antidiscrimination law and minority employment: Recruitment practices and regulatory constraints.* Chicago: University of Chicago Press.

Carnevale, A. P. (1991). *America and the new economy: How new competitive standards are radically changing American workplaces.* San Francisco: Jossey-Bass.

Carnevale, A. P., & Carnevale, E. S. (1994). Growth patterns in workplace training. *Training & Development Journal, 48*(5), S22–S32.

Cetron, M. (1994). An American renaissance in the year 2000. *The Futurist, 28,* 1–12.

Forrest, M. R. (1995). 'Walkin' your talk,' or moving along the road to workplace diversity. *Journal of Career Planning & Employment, 55*(2), 3.

Hopkins, K. R., Nestleroth, S. L., & Bolick, C. (1991). *Help wanted: How companies can survive and thrive in the coming worker shortage.* New York: McGraw-Hill.

Jamieson, D., & O'Mara, J. (1991). *Managing workforce 2000: Gaining the diversity advantage.* San Francisco: Jossey-Bass.

Johnson, O., Dailey, V. (Eds.). (1994). *The 1994 information please almanac.* Boston: Houghton Mifflin.

Mahar, M. (1993). The truth about women's pay. *Working Woman, 18,* 52–55, 100–103.

Martinez, M. N. (1995). Poor advancement opportunities for minorities. *HRMagazine,* 40(2), 14–16.

Potter, E. E. & Youngman, J. A. (1995). *Keeping America competitive: Employment policy for the twenty-first century.* Lakewood, CO: Glenbridge Publishing.

Reynolds, L. (1994). Business realities clash with training needs and turnover. *HR Focus,* 71(1), 1, 8.

Secretary's Commission on Achieving Necessary Skills. (1992). *Skills and tasks for jobs: A SCANS report for America 2000.* Washington, D.C.: U.S. Government Printing Office.

Snelling, R. O. (1987). *The right job.* New York: Viking Press.

U.S. Department of Labor. (Spring 1992). *Occupational Outlook Quarterly.* Washington, D.C.: U.S. Government Printing Office.

U.S. Department of Labor. (1993). *Current Population Survey.* Washington, D.C.: U.S. Government Printing Office.

U.S. Department of Labor. (October 1993). *Monthly Labor Review.* Washington, D.C.: U.S. Government Printing Office.

U.S. Department of Labor. (November 1993). *Monthly Labor Review.* Washington, D.C.: U.S. Government Printing Office.

U.S. Department of Labor. (Fall 1993). *Occupational Outlook Quarterly.* Washington, D.C.: U.S. Government Printing Office.

U.S. Department of Labor. (1994a). *Employment in perspective: Minority workers.* (Report No. 874). Washington, D.C.: U.S. Government Printing Office.

U.S. Department of Labor. (1994b). *Employment in perspective: Women in the labor force.* (Report No. 872). Washington, D.C.: U.S. Government Printing Office.

U.S. Department of Labor. (July 1994). *Monthly Labor Review.* Washington, D.C.: U.S. Government Printing Office.

U.S. Department of Labor. (1994–1995). *Occupational Outlook Handbook.* Washington, D.C.: U.S. Government Printing Office.

Wells, R. M. & Idelson, H. (1995). Panel will examine effects of affirmative action. *Congressional Quarterly, 53*(11), 819–820.

Chapter 3

American Heritage Dictionary (1985). Boston: Houghton Mifflin.

Baier, J. L., & Strong, T. S. (1994). *Technology in student affairs: issues, applications, and trends.* Washington, D.C.: American College Personnel Association.

Burton, M. L., & Wedemeyer, R. A. (1991). *In Transition.* New York: HarperBusiness.

Fisher, R. B. (1984). Career navigation: Another perspective on career planning. *Journal of College Placement, 84,* 26–28.

Parsons, F. (1909). *Choosing a vocation.* Boston: Houghton Mifflin.

Chapter 4

Isaacson, L. E., & Brown, D. (1993). *Career information, career counseling, and career development* (5th ed.). Boston: Allyn and Bacon.

Chapter 5

Borchard, D. C., Kelly, J. J., & Weaver, N. K. (1992). *Your career: Choices, chances, changes* (5th ed.). Dubuque, IA: Kendall/Hunt.

Fisher, R. B. (1984). Career navigation: Another perspective on career planning. *Journal of College Placement, 84,* 26–28.

Krumboltz, J. D., Rude, S. S., Mitchell, L. K., Hamel, D. A., & Kinnier, R. T. (1982). Behaviors associated with "good" and "poor" outcomes in a simulated career decision. *Journal of Vocational Behavior, 21*(3), 349–358.

Mitchell, A., Jones, G. B., & Krumboltz, J. D. (1979). *Social learning and career decision making.* Cranston, RI: Carroll Press.

Chapter 6

Gordon, J. (Ed.). (1994). Whining about the skills gap. *Training, 31*(1), 14.

Ramsey, R. D. (1994). How to hire the best. *Supervision, 55* (4), 14–17.

Secretary's Commission on Achieving Necessary Skills. (1992). *Skills and tasks for jobs: A SCANS report for America 2000.* Washington, D.C.: U.S. Government Printing Office.

White, B. J. (1994). Developing leaders for the high-performance workplace. *Human Resource Management, 33* (1), 161–168.

Chapter 7

Kennedy, J. L., Murrow, T. J. (1994). *The electronic resume revolution: Creating a winning resume for the new world of job seeking.* New York: John Wiley & Sons.

Chapter 10

Bolles, R. (1995). *What color is your parachute?: A practical manual for job hunters and career changers.* Berkeley, CA: Ten Speed Press.

Powell, C. R. (1990). *Career planning today* (2nd ed.). Dubuque, IA: Kendall/Hunt.

Snelling, R. O. (1987). *The Right Job.* New York: Viking Press.

Chapter 11

Ireland, Karin (1994). *The job survival instruction book.* Hawthorne, NJ: Career Press.

Koonce, R. (1995). Becoming your own career coach. *Training & Development, 49* (1), 18–25.

Steele, J. E., & Morgan, M. S. (1991). *Career planning and development for college students and recent graduates.* Lincolnwood, IL: NTC Publishing Group.

Author Index

Subject Index